Journalism Ethics and Challenges

C. P. Kumar
Reiki Healer & Author
Roorkee - 247667, India

Disclaimer

While every effort has been made to ensure the accuracy and completeness of the content in this book, the author cannot guarantee that the information contained herein is error-free, up-to-date, or suitable for every individual circumstance.

The author shall not be held liable or responsible for any errors or omissions in the content of the book, nor for any damages, or losses that may arise from any actions taken based upon the suggestions or contents presented in the book.

Readers are advised to use their own judgment and discretion in applying the information provided in this book, and to consult with qualified professionals before taking any action based on the contents of this book. The author disclaims any and all liability or responsibility for any actions taken or not taken based on the information contained in this book.

DEDICATION

To the tireless guardians of truth, the dedicated journalists who navigate the complex landscapes of information, we dedicate this book.

In a world where the pursuit of veracity and integrity faces unprecedented challenges, you stand as the vanguards of ethics in journalism. To those who tirelessly seek the truth, inform the public, and educate society, this work is dedicated to you.

May the insights within these pages serve as a guiding light through the intricate realm of Journalism Ethics. Your commitment to the principles outlined in these chapters - from the importance of truth and integrity to the challenges posed by evolving technologies, biases, and the changing media landscape - embodies the essence of responsible journalism.

In recognition of your unwavering dedication to protecting sources, avoiding conflicts of interest, and maintaining objectivity, we salute your commitment to the ethics of news gathering. Your courageous pursuit of investigative journalism, your role in upholding press freedom, and your vital contributions to democracy do not go unnoticed.

As you navigate the diverse and evolving field of journalism, from the challenges of international reporting to the ethical considerations in crisis and trauma reporting, may this book serve as a resource, providing insights and ethical frameworks to guide your path.

To those who contribute to the rich tapestry of journalism, including opinion writers, photojournalists, and those addressing diversity and sensitive topics, we extend our appreciation for your commitment to balanced and responsible expression.

In recognizing the challenges you face, from the business aspects of journalism to the responsibilities in data journalism, collaborative efforts, and media literacy education, this dedication stands as a tribute to your resilience and dedication.

To the future of journalism, we dedicate the concluding chapter. May it inspire reflection on the role you play in society, the impact you have on communities, and the responsibility you bear in shaping the narratives that define our shared reality.

This dedication is a heartfelt tribute to all journalists, past, present, and future, who embody the principles of truth, integrity, and ethical journalism. May your pens remain mighty, your voices resolute, and your commitment to journalistic ethics unwavering.

With deep respect and gratitude,

C. P. Kumar

CONTENTS

PREFACE

In the ever-evolving landscape of news dissemination, the role of journalism remains paramount in shaping public discourse, fostering transparency, and holding power to account. This book, "Journalism Ethics and Challenges", delves into the ethical considerations and multifaceted challenges faced by journalists in an era marked by technological advancements, information overload, and shifting societal expectations.

The journey begins with an exploration, highlighting the foundational principles of journalism ethics, emphasizing the enduring importance of truth and integrity. As we progress through the subsequent chapters, readers will gain insights into the pivotal role journalism plays in society and trace the historical trajectory of this noble profession from the print era to the digital age.

The book addresses the transformative impact of technology on journalism, scrutinizing the rise of social media, artificial intelligence, and the implications for the future of news. It delves into the complexities of digital literacy and misinformation, exploring the challenges of navigating an information landscape where truth can be elusive.

Challenges facing journalism today take center stage, examining issues such as bias, credibility, and the seismic shifts in traditional media. The subsequent chapters dive into the intricacies of ethical news gathering, whistleblower protection, and the rigorous demands of investigative journalism.

Beyond the national borders, the book explores the challenges of international reporting, addressing safety concerns, security issues, and the nuances of cultural differences. Press freedom and censorship take the spotlight, underscoring the ongoing struggle for the right to report without restraint.

The book also ventures into specialized domains such as environmental journalism, opinion writing, and photojournalism, shedding light on the unique ethical considerations within these spheres. Issues of diversity, media literacy education, and the business side of journalism are examined, providing a comprehensive view of the contemporary media landscape.

The concluding chapters navigate the uncharted territories of crisis reporting, trauma-informed journalism, and the responsibilities journalists bear in covering sensitive topics. Finally, the book reflects on the future of journalism, considering its evolving role in society and the ethical imperatives that will shape its trajectory.

"Journalism Ethics and Challenges" is not merely a collection of chapters but a mosaic that reflects the diverse facets of journalism. It serves as a compass for journalists, educators, students, and anyone intrigued by the profound impact of responsible and ethical journalism on society. As we embark on this journey, let us explore the ethical nuances that underpin the noble pursuit of truth in an ever-changing media landscape.

C. P. Kumar
Reiki Healer & Author
Web: https://www.angelfire.com/nh/cpkumar/virgo.html

Chapter 1. Introduction to Journalism Ethics
The Importance of Truth and Integrity

Introduction

In the ever-evolving landscape of journalism, the ethical principles that guide the profession are more crucial than ever. Journalists play a pivotal role in shaping public opinion, influencing societal discourse, and holding those in power accountable. As the guardians of truth and integrity, journalists are entrusted with the responsibility of delivering accurate and unbiased information to the public. This article delves into the foundational principles of journalism ethics, with a specific focus on the paramount importance of truth and integrity in the field.

The Historical Context of Journalism Ethics

To understand the contemporary significance of journalism ethics, it is essential to trace its roots back to the historical development of the profession. The concept of journalistic ethics has evolved alongside the growth of mass media and the increasing influence of the press. From the advent of newspapers in the 17th century to the emergence of radio, television, and digital media, the ethical standards guiding journalism have adapted to the changing landscape.

The Role of Truth in Journalism

At the heart of journalism ethics lies the commitment to truth. Journalists are expected to provide the public with accurate and reliable information, serving as a watchdog against misinformation and propaganda. The pursuit of truth requires thorough research, fact-checking, and a dedication to presenting an unbiased account of events. In a world inundated with fake news and sensationalism, the adherence to truth remains the bedrock of responsible journalism.

Challenges to Truth in the Digital Age

In the contemporary digital age, the challenges to upholding truth in journalism have become more complex. The rapid dissemination of information through social media, the rise of citizen journalism, and the pressure for instant news coverage have all contributed to an environment where misinformation can spread unchecked. *Citizen journalism* refers to the collection, reporting, and dissemination of news and information by individuals who are not professional journalists but contribute to news coverage through digital platforms and social media. Journalists now face the challenge of navigating a landscape where the line between news and opinion is often blurred, making the pursuit of truth a constant battle against the tide of misinformation.

The Impact of Integrity on Journalism

Integrity, in the context of journalism ethics, refers to the commitment to fairness, impartiality, and transparency. Journalists are expected to conduct themselves with honesty and uphold the highest standards of professionalism. Maintaining integrity is not only crucial for building and preserving public trust but also for ensuring that journalism fulfills its democratic function of informing and empowering the public.

Balancing Objectivity and Subjectivity

Objectivity refers to the quality of being impartial, unbiased, and free from personal opinions or emotions, while subjectivity refers to the presence of personal opinions, feelings, and perspectives in a manner that may not be universally verifiable or agreed upon.

One of the perennial challenges in journalism ethics is striking the delicate balance between objectivity and subjectivity. While journalists are expected to report the facts objectively, they are also human beings with their own perspectives and biases. Navigating this fine line requires self-awareness, editorial oversight, and a commitment to presenting a diversity of voices and opinions. The ability to maintain objectivity while acknowledging inherent subjectivities is a testament to a journalist's integrity.

Navigating Conflicts of Interest

Integrity in journalism is often tested when journalists find themselves facing potential conflicts of interest. Whether it's financial interests, personal relationships, or affiliations with certain groups, journalists must navigate these challenges transparently. Disclosing potential conflicts of interest is an essential step in maintaining the public's trust and ensuring that journalistic endeavors remain untainted by external influences.

Ethical Decision-Making in Journalism

The ethical dilemmas that journalists encounter require a thoughtful and principled approach to decision-making. Ethical guidelines, established by journalistic organizations and institutions, serve as a compass for navigating these challenges. The Society of Professional Journalists (United States), for example, emphasizes the importance of seeking the truth, minimizing harm, acting independently, and being accountable and transparent. Ethical decision-making in journalism involves a constant evaluation of the potential impact of one's actions on the public and the profession.

The Accountability of Journalists

Accountability is a cornerstone of journalistic integrity. Journalists are accountable not only to their audiences but also to the subjects of their stories and the broader community. Inaccuracies and misrepresentations can have far-reaching consequences, eroding trust in the media and undermining the democratic function of journalism. Acknowledging mistakes, issuing corrections, and learning from errors are vital aspects of maintaining accountability in journalism.

Press Freedom and Responsibility

While journalistic freedom is essential for a thriving democracy, it comes with a corresponding responsibility to the public. The power of the press to shape opinions and influence public discourse requires a commitment to ethical standards. Press freedom is not a license for irresponsible journalism; instead, it demands a heightened sense of responsibility in wielding the influence that comes with the Fourth Estate.

The *Fourth Estate* traditionally refers to the news media or journalism as a collective and influential force in society that operates independently of the government, executive, legislative, and judicial branches. The term highlights the media's role as a check on government power and its ability to inform the public, acting as a "fourth" institution alongside the three branches of government. The *three branches* of government (executive, legislative, and judicial) respectively implement and enforce laws, make laws, and interpret laws in democratic systems.

The Evolving Landscape of Journalism Ethics

As technology continues to reshape the media landscape, journalism ethics must evolve to meet new challenges. The advent of artificial intelligence, deepfake technology, and algorithm-driven content distribution poses ethical questions that demand careful consideration. *Deepfake technology* involves the use of artificial intelligence (AI) to create highly realistic and often deceptive multimedia content, such as videos or audio recordings, that depict individuals saying or doing things they did not actually say or do. The responsibility to remain ethical in the face of these challenges rests on both individual journalists and the broader media industry.

Conclusion

Journalism ethics, with a focus on truth and integrity, is indispensable for the credibility and effectiveness of the media. The historical context of journalistic ethics, the role of truth in journalism, challenges in the digital age, and the impact of integrity on journalistic practices all contribute to the complex tapestry of ethical considerations in the field. As journalism continues to evolve, maintaining a commitment to truth and integrity ensures that the profession fulfills its vital role in fostering an informed and empowered society. The ongoing conversation about journalism ethics and challenges is essential for navigating the intricate intersection of media, democracy, and ethical responsibility.

Chapter 2. The Role of Journalism in Society
Investigating, Informing, and Educating the Public

Introduction

In an era characterized by rapid technological advancements and evolving communication landscapes, journalism remains a cornerstone of societal progress. The role of journalism transcends mere information dissemination; it is a powerful force that investigates, informs, and educates the public. This article delves into the multifaceted aspects of journalism, exploring its ethical considerations, challenges, and its indispensable contribution to the well-being of a democratic society.

Investigating the Truth

1. Unearthing Hidden Realities

Journalism, at its core, is about uncovering truths that may be concealed or distorted. Investigative journalism plays a pivotal role in scrutinizing issues that impact society. Investigative reporters act as watchdogs, delving deep into complex matters to expose corruption, injustice, and other societal maladies. Their work serves as a check and balance on power, fostering accountability in both public and private spheres.

2. Navigating Ethical Dilemmas

However, the pursuit of truth in journalism is not without its ethical challenges. Journalists must navigate a delicate balance between the public's right to know and the potential harm that sensitive information may cause. Striking this balance requires careful consideration of the ethical principles that underpin responsible journalism, such as accuracy, fairness, and minimizing harm.

Informing the Public

1. The Information Ecosystem

In a world inundated with information, journalism acts as a filter, distilling complex events into comprehensible narratives. Journalists curate and prioritize information, ensuring that the public is informed about critical issues that shape society. This function is particularly crucial in an age of misinformation, where discerning the truth from falsehood is a formidable challenge.

2. Holding Power Accountable

Beyond merely providing information, journalism holds those in power accountable for their actions. Through investigative reporting and critical analysis, journalists expose malfeasance and shine a light on issues that demand public attention. This accountability function is integral to the democratic process, as an informed citizenry is essential for the proper functioning of democratic institutions.

Educating the Public

1. Facilitating Informed Decision-Making

Education is a fundamental pillar of journalism, empowering individuals to make informed decisions about their lives and communities. Journalists play the role of educators, breaking down complex subjects, and presenting them in a manner accessible to the general public. In doing so, they contribute to the development of an informed and engaged citizenry.

2. Fostering Civic Participation

Journalism fosters civic participation by providing the information necessary for citizens to engage meaningfully in the democratic process. Through in-depth reporting on political issues, societal challenges, and policy debates, journalists enable citizens to participate actively in shaping the direction of their communities and nations.

Ethical Considerations in Journalism

1. Balancing Objectivity and Advocacy

Objectivity involves presenting information without bias or personal opinions, while advocacy is the active support or promotion of a particular cause, often expressing a point of view. The former aims for impartiality, while the latter involves taking a position and actively supporting it.

One of the perennial ethical challenges in journalism is striking the right balance between objectivity and advocacy. While journalists are expected to report facts without bias, they also have a responsibility to highlight injustices and champion social causes. Navigating this delicate balance requires a nuanced understanding of journalistic ethics.

2. Handling Sensitive Information

Journalists often grapple with the dilemma of handling sensitive information, especially when it involves the private lives of individuals. The ethical obligation to minimize harm clashes with the public's desire for transparency. Journalistic codes of ethics provide guidelines, but real-world situations demand careful consideration of the potential consequences of publishing sensitive information.

Challenges Facing Contemporary Journalism

1. Digital Disruption

The advent of the digital age has disrupted traditional journalism models, presenting both opportunities and challenges. While digital platforms enable wider reach, they also give rise to issues such as misinformation, clickbait, and the erosion of traditional revenue models. *Clickbait* refers to content, typically in online articles or social media posts, that uses sensationalized or misleading headlines and thumbnails to attract clicks and views, often with the goal of increasing advertising revenue or web traffic. Navigating this landscape requires adaptability and a commitment to upholding journalistic standards.

2. Threats to Press Freedom

Journalists often find themselves in precarious situations, facing threats to their safety and press freedom. Whether it be intimidation, censorship, or physical harm, journalists must navigate these challenges to fulfill their role as society's watchdogs. International collaboration and advocacy for press freedom become essential in safeguarding the integrity of journalism.

The Future of Journalism

1. Embracing Innovation

The future of journalism lies in embracing technological innovations while upholding ethical standards. From immersive storytelling techniques to data journalism, new tools offer journalists opportunities to engage audiences in novel ways. However, ethical considerations must remain at the forefront to ensure that innovation enhances rather than compromises the integrity of journalism.

2. Reinforcing Media Literacy

As misinformation proliferates, media literacy becomes a critical skill for the public. Journalists bear the responsibility of reinforcing media literacy through transparent reporting, fact-checking, and providing context. By empowering the audience to critically evaluate information, journalism can contribute to building a more discerning and informed society.

Conclusion

Journalism, as the Fourth Estate, plays an irreplaceable role in the fabric of democratic societies. Through investigating the truth, informing the public, and educating citizens, journalists contribute to the health and vibrancy of democratic institutions. However, this noble endeavor is not without its ethical challenges and external threats. As journalism evolves in the face of technological advancements, maintaining a commitment to truth, accountability, and public service remains paramount. The future of journalism hinges on its ability to adapt, innovate responsibly, and uphold the ethical principles that underpin its indispensable role in society.

Chapter 3. The History of Journalism
From Print to Digital Media

Introduction

The history of journalism is a fascinating journey that spans centuries, reflecting the evolution of human communication and the dissemination of information. From its humble beginnings in handwritten manuscripts to the digital age, journalism has undergone profound transformations, adapting to the changing needs and technologies of society. This article delves into the rich tapestry of journalism, tracing its trajectory from print to digital media, exploring the ethical challenges that have emerged along the way.

Early Origins: Manuscripts and Pamphlets

Journalism's roots can be traced back to ancient civilizations where scribes documented events on clay tablets. However, the true advent of journalism as we recognize it today began with the invention of the printing press in the 15th century. The Gutenberg press revolutionized the dissemination of information, enabling the mass production of newspapers and pamphlets. This marked the birth of print journalism, allowing news to reach a broader audience than ever before.

The Rise of Newspapers

The 17th century witnessed the establishment of the first regular newspapers in Europe, with publications like The London Gazette and The Oxford Gazette. These newspapers were often controlled by governments and served as mouthpieces for political propaganda. However, as the 18th century unfolded, the press began to assert its independence. Journalists embraced the concept of a free press as a cornerstone of democracy, paving the way for investigative journalism and the pursuit of truth.

The Yellow Journalism Era

The late 19th century saw the rise of "yellow journalism" in the United States, characterized by sensationalism, exaggeration, and eye-catching headlines. Newspapers engaged in fierce competition for readership, often prioritizing entertainment over accuracy. While this era contributed to the growth of circulation numbers, it also raised ethical concerns about journalistic integrity and the responsible use of media influence.

Wire Services and Globalization

The turn of the 20th century introduced wire services like the Associated Press (American news agency) and Reuters (British news agency), enabling newspapers to access news from around the world. This marked a significant shift towards globalization in journalism, as information could now be disseminated internationally in near-real-time. However, the reliance on wire services also raised concerns about homogenization and the potential for biased reporting.

Broadcast Journalism: Radio and Television

The mid-20th century brought about a new era with the advent of broadcast journalism. Radio and television became powerful mediums for storytelling, allowing journalists to convey news with immediacy and impact. The iconic voices of radio and the familiar faces on television became trusted sources of information for the public. However, the visual and auditory nature of broadcast journalism posed new challenges, as the medium's persuasive elements could influence public opinion more profoundly.

Digital Revolution: The Internet Age

The late 20th century witnessed the transformative impact of the internet on journalism. The World Wide Web became a democratizing force, allowing individuals to publish and access information without traditional gatekeepers. The rise of online news portals and blogs challenged the dominance of traditional media outlets, ushering in an era of decentralization and diversification.

Challenges of the Digital Age: Speed vs. Accuracy

The digital age brought about a paradigm shift in journalism dynamics. The demand for real-time news updates in a 24/7 news cycle led to a trade-off between speed and accuracy. Journalists faced the challenge of delivering news quickly while ensuring factual correctness. The pressure to be the first to break a story sometimes compromised the thorough fact-checking processes that print journalism had historically upheld.

Social Media and Citizen Journalism

The advent of social media platforms further altered the landscape of journalism. Platforms like Twitter and Facebook became conduits for citizen journalism, enabling individuals to share news and opinions in real-time. While this democratization of information was empowering, it also gave rise to concerns about misinformation and the lack of editorial oversight. The viral spread of unverified news became a significant ethical challenge for journalists and media organizations.

Monetization Pressures and Clickbait

As digital journalism expanded, monetization became a pressing concern. Ad-driven revenue models incentivized the production of click-worthy content, leading to the rise of clickbait headlines and sensationalism. The prioritization of audience engagement over journalistic values raised ethical questions about the industry's responsibility to inform and educate rather than simply entertain.

Data Privacy and Investigative Journalism

The digital age also brought forth ethical challenges related to data privacy. Investigative journalism, while empowered by digital tools, faced dilemmas concerning the responsible handling of sensitive information. The tension between the public's right to know and the protection of individuals' privacy became a central theme in debates over journalistic ethics.

Fake News and Information Manipulation

One of the most significant ethical challenges of the digital era is the proliferation of fake news and information manipulation. The ease with which false information can spread online has raised questions about the role of journalists in verifying and debunking information. The need for media literacy and critical thinking has become paramount as society grapples with the challenge of distinguishing fact from fiction.

Conclusion

The history of journalism from print to digital media is a tale of adaptation and evolution. As technology continues to advance, journalists must grapple with new ethical challenges while upholding the principles that form the foundation of their profession. Navigating the complex landscape of the digital age requires a commitment to truth, accuracy, and the public interest. As journalism moves forward, the lessons of its history will serve as a guide, reminding practitioners of the enduring importance of ethical conduct in the pursuit of an informed and engaged society.

Chapter 4. The Impact of Technology on Journalism
Social Media, AI, and the Future of News

Introduction

The landscape of journalism has undergone a profound transformation in recent years, primarily driven by advancements in technology. The rise of social media platforms and the integration of artificial intelligence (AI) into news production and dissemination have reshaped the way information is gathered, reported, and consumed. As we navigate this digital era, it becomes imperative to examine the ethical considerations and challenges that accompany these technological shifts in journalism.

The Social Media Revolution

Social media platforms have emerged as powerful tools that not only connect individuals globally but also serve as platforms for news dissemination. The instantaneous nature of platforms like Twitter and Facebook has allowed journalists to report on events as they unfold, breaking news in real-time. However, this immediacy has also given rise to challenges such as misinformation, clickbait, and the erosion of traditional editorial processes.

1. Real-time Reporting and Citizen Journalism

The advent of social media has democratized journalism, enabling ordinary citizens to participate in news reporting. The prevalence of citizen journalism has both positive and negative implications. On the one hand, it allows for diverse perspectives and eyewitness accounts. On the other hand, it raises concerns about the accuracy and reliability of information, as user-generated content may lack the editorial scrutiny applied by professional journalists.

2. Misinformation and Clickbait

The viral nature of social media can amplify the spread of misinformation, leading to the rapid dissemination of false or misleading narratives. The pressure for clicks and engagement has incentivized the creation of clickbait headlines, compromising journalistic integrity. Journalists must navigate the fine line between capturing audience attention and delivering accurate, unbiased information.

Artificial Intelligence in Journalism

The integration of AI in journalism has ushered in a new era of efficiency and automation, with applications ranging from content creation to audience engagement. While AI technologies offer promising solutions, they also present ethical dilemmas and challenges that demand careful consideration.

1. Automated Content Creation

AI-driven tools, such as natural language processing algorithms, are increasingly being used to generate news articles and reports. While these technologies can enhance efficiency, they raise concerns about the potential loss of human nuance and the risk of biased content. Journalists must grapple with the ethical implications of relying on machines for content creation and balance the advantages with the need for human oversight.

2. Personalized News and Filter Bubbles

AI algorithms play a crucial role in curating personalized news feeds for individuals based on their preferences and behavior. While this enhances user experience, it also contributes to the formation of filter bubbles - echo chambers where individuals are exposed only to information that aligns with their existing beliefs. Journalists must confront the challenge of delivering diverse perspectives in an era where algorithms cater to individual preferences, potentially reinforcing bias and limiting exposure to differing opinions.

The Ethical Imperatives

As technology reshapes the journalism landscape, ethical considerations become paramount. Journalists must navigate a complex terrain, balancing the demands of immediacy and engagement with the principles of accuracy, fairness, and accountability.

1. Transparency and Accountability

In the era of social media and AI, maintaining transparency is essential for building trust with the audience. Journalists should disclose their sources, methodologies, and any potential conflicts of interest. Additionally, as AI tools are employed in newsrooms, the responsibility for the ethical use of these technologies falls on both journalists and the organizations employing them.

2. Combatting Misinformation

The prevalence of misinformation underscores the need for journalists to be vigilant gatekeepers of truth. Fact-checking, verifying sources, and resisting the temptation to prioritize speed over accuracy are crucial ethical imperatives. Collaborative efforts between news organizations, fact-checking entities, and social media platforms are essential to curbing the spread of false information.

3. Balancing Technology and Human Judgment

While technology offers unprecedented tools for efficiency and innovation, human judgment remains irreplaceable in ethical decision-making. Journalists must resist the allure of automation and AI without thoughtful consideration of the ethical implications. The editorial process should involve a balance between technological advancements and the nuanced judgment that human journalists bring to the table.

The Future of Journalism

Looking ahead, the future of journalism lies at the intersection of technological innovation and ethical resilience. Navigating the evolving landscape requires a proactive approach that harnesses the benefits of technology while safeguarding the principles that underpin ethical journalism.

1. Digital Literacy and Media Education

As technology continues to evolve, enhancing digital literacy becomes imperative for both journalists and the audience. Media education programs can empower individuals to critically evaluate information, discern between credible and unreliable sources, and understand the ethical considerations involved in news production. Journalists, in turn, should prioritize clear communication and accessibility in their reporting to facilitate understanding.

2. Collaboration and Industry Standards

The challenges posed by technology require collaborative efforts within the journalism industry. Establishing and adhering to industry-wide standards for the ethical use of technology can provide a framework for responsible journalism. Collaborations between journalists, technologists, and policymakers can lead to the development of guidelines that prioritize ethical considerations and ensure the responsible integration of technology in newsrooms.

Conclusion

The impact of technology on journalism is a dynamic and ongoing narrative. From the rapid dissemination of news on social media platforms to the integration of AI in news production, the ethical challenges and considerations are both complex and pressing. Journalists must navigate this terrain with a commitment to transparency, accuracy, and accountability, ensuring that technology serves as an ally rather than a threat to the foundational principles of ethical journalism. As we forge ahead into the future, the symbiotic relationship between technology and ethical journalism will play a pivotal role in shaping the information landscape for generations to come.

Chapter 5. Digital Literacy and Misinformation
Navigating Challenges in the Information Age

Introduction

In the contemporary landscape of journalism, the rapid proliferation of digital platforms has transformed the way information is disseminated and consumed. The rise of the internet and social media has provided unprecedented access to information, but it has also ushered in new challenges, particularly concerning digital literacy and the prevalence of misinformation. This article explores the intricate relationship between digital literacy and misinformation, delving into the challenges journalists face in navigating this complex terrain.

Understanding Digital Literacy

Digital literacy encompasses the skills and knowledge required to critically engage with digital technologies and effectively navigate the digital landscape. In the context of journalism, digital literacy is a fundamental tool for reporters and media professionals to adapt to the evolving nature of their industry. This includes the ability to evaluate online sources, discern credible information from misinformation, and understand the implications of digital tools on the dissemination of news.

The Evolving Role of Journalists

As gatekeepers of information, journalists play a pivotal role in shaping public opinion. However, the digital age has disrupted traditional journalism models, challenging the established norms of fact-checking and source verification. In the era of instant news and user-generated content, journalists must adapt their practices to maintain the integrity of their profession while keeping pace with the rapid dissemination of information on digital platforms.

The Proliferation of Misinformation

One of the primary challenges journalists face in the digital age is the rampant spread of misinformation. The ease with which false or misleading information can be disseminated online poses a significant threat to the credibility of journalism. Social media platforms, in particular, serve as breeding grounds for the viral spread of misinformation, as sensationalized content often gains more traction than accurate reporting.

The Role of Social Media

Social media platforms, such as Facebook and Twitter, have become powerful tools for the dissemination of news. However, they also serve as fertile grounds for the rapid spread of misinformation. The lack of editorial oversight on these platforms allows misinformation to circulate unchecked, reaching a vast audience before corrective measures can be implemented. Journalists must navigate this challenging landscape, finding ways to harness the benefits of social media while mitigating the risks associated with misinformation.

Challenges in Identifying Misinformation

Identifying misinformation is a nuanced task that requires a combination of traditional journalistic skills and digital literacy. False information often mimics the format and style of legitimate news, making it challenging for both journalists and the general public to discern fact from fiction. The speed at which information spreads online further complicates the process of verifying sources and ensuring the accuracy of news stories.

The Echo Chamber Effect

Social media algorithms often contribute to the formation of echo chambers, where users are exposed to information that aligns with their pre-existing beliefs and opinions. This selective exposure can reinforce misinformation, as individuals are more likely to accept and share content that confirms their biases. Journalists must grapple with the challenge of breaking through these echo chambers to present a more balanced and accurate representation of events.

Addressing Digital Literacy Gaps

To combat the spread of misinformation, there is an urgent need to address digital literacy gaps within society. Journalists can play a pivotal role in promoting media literacy by creating content that educates the public on how to critically evaluate information online. News organizations should collaborate with educators to integrate digital literacy into school curricula, fostering a generation of individuals equipped to navigate the complexities of the digital age.

Media Literacy Initiatives

Media literacy initiatives can serve as a proactive approach to mitigating the impact of misinformation. By promoting critical thinking skills and teaching individuals how to verify information, these initiatives empower the public to be discerning consumers of news. Journalists, in collaboration with educational institutions and advocacy groups, can contribute to the development and implementation of media literacy programs that address the unique challenges posed by the digital landscape.

Fact-Checking in the Digital Age

Fact-checking involves verifying and assessing the accuracy of information, statements, or claims to ensure they are supported by evidence and adhere to objective standards of truth and accuracy. Fact-checking has become an indispensable tool in the journalist's toolkit to combat misinformation. With the rise of digital platforms, fact-checking initiatives have expanded their reach, debunking false claims and correcting inaccuracies in real-time. Journalists must embrace fact-checking as an integral part of their reporting process, leveraging technology to swiftly identify and rectify misinformation before it gains widespread traction.

The Role of Artificial Intelligence

Artificial Intelligence (AI) technologies, including machine learning algorithms, can be employed to enhance the efficiency of fact-checking processes. These tools can analyze large datasets, identify patterns of misinformation, and assist journalists in verifying the authenticity of sources. However, the ethical implications of relying on AI in journalism raise concerns about bias and the potential for algorithmic errors, necessitating a careful and transparent integration of these technologies into newsrooms.

Collaboration between Social Media Platforms and News Organizations

Addressing misinformation requires collaboration between social media platforms and news organizations. While platforms must take responsibility for curbing the spread of false information on their sites, news organizations can contribute by establishing partnerships with digital platforms to promote verified and credible content. This collaborative approach can involve the development of algorithms that prioritize reliable sources and the implementation of tools to flag or limit the reach of potentially misleading information.

Transparency in Journalism

Maintaining trust in journalism is essential in the face of rampant misinformation. Transparency about the journalistic process, including source verification and fact-checking procedures, can help build credibility with audiences. Journalists should be proactive in explaining their methods and acknowledging any errors, reinforcing the commitment to accuracy and accountability. Open communication with the public fosters a sense of trust and encourages a more critical and discerning readership.

Conclusion

In the information age, the challenges posed by digital literacy and misinformation are intricately woven into the fabric of journalism. Navigating this complex landscape requires a multifaceted approach, encompassing the development of digital literacy skills, proactive media literacy initiatives, and the responsible integration of technology. Journalists, as guardians of truth, must adapt to the evolving nature of their profession, leveraging their expertise to combat misinformation while upholding the principles of accuracy, transparency, and accountability in the pursuit of ethical journalism. As we continue to grapple with the dynamics of the digital age, the role of journalists in fostering a digitally literate and well-informed society remains more crucial than ever.

Chapter 6. Challenges Facing Journalism Today
Bias, Credibility, and the Decline of Traditional Media

Introduction

In the dynamic landscape of contemporary journalism, the profession faces a myriad of challenges that shape the way information is disseminated and consumed. This article explores three critical challenges confronting journalism today: Bias, Credibility, and the Decline of Traditional Media. As the Fourth Estate, journalism plays a pivotal role in a democratic society, providing citizens with accurate and reliable information. However, the evolving media landscape, coupled with technological advancements, has introduced complexities that demand a closer examination of ethical considerations and professional standards.

Bias in Journalism

One of the foremost challenges facing journalism in the 21st century is the pervasive issue of bias. Journalists are entrusted with the responsibility of presenting information in an objective and unbiased manner, allowing the public to form their opinions based on a fair representation of facts. However, the reality often falls short of this ideal, as various forms of bias infiltrate news reporting.

Political Bias

Political bias is perhaps the most prevalent form of bias in journalism today. In an era of heightened political polarization, media outlets are increasingly associated with particular ideologies, influencing the way news stories are framed and presented. The rise of partisan news sources has exacerbated this issue, with audiences often gravitating towards outlets that align with their pre-existing beliefs, creating echo chambers that reinforce biases.

Economic Bias

Economic considerations also contribute to bias in journalism. Media organizations, reliant on advertising revenue, may be influenced by the interests of their sponsors. This economic pressure can compromise editorial independence, leading to self-censorship or the downplaying of stories that may be detrimental to financial interests. The pursuit of ratings and clicks in the digital age further intensifies this challenge, as sensationalism and clickbait strategies can compromise the integrity of news reporting.

Cultural and Social Bias

Cultural and social biases can manifest in various forms, from gender and racial biases to regional or class-based prejudices. Journalists, consciously or unconsciously, may bring their own perspectives and experiences into their reporting, affecting how events are portrayed. This challenge highlights the importance of diversity in newsrooms, ensuring a broader range of voices and perspectives are represented in the media landscape.

Addressing Bias: The Role of Media Literacy

To combat bias in journalism, there is a growing need for media literacy initiatives. Educating the public on how to critically evaluate news sources and recognize different forms of bias can empower individuals to navigate the complex media landscape. Additionally, media organizations should invest in diversity and inclusion efforts within their newsrooms to mitigate cultural and social biases, fostering a more nuanced and representative journalism.

Credibility Crisis in Journalism

Closely linked to the issue of bias is the credibility crisis that journalism is currently grappling with. The proliferation of misinformation, the rise of fake news, and the erosion of trust in traditional media outlets have created a challenging environment for journalists seeking to uphold the principles of accuracy and truthfulness.

Misinformation and Fake News

The digital age has facilitated the rapid spread of misinformation, fueled by the ease with which false narratives can be disseminated through social media platforms. The viral nature of such information poses a significant threat to the credibility of journalism, as falsehoods can gain traction faster than corrections can be made. The lack of gatekeeping in the online space allows for the unchecked proliferation of fake news, undermining the public's confidence in the veracity of news sources.

Erosion of Trust in Traditional Media

Traditional media outlets, once considered bastions of reliable information, have faced a decline in public trust. The perception of bias, sensationalism, and the perceived prioritization of entertainment over news has led to a skepticism that extends beyond partisan lines. The erosion of trust in mainstream media has created a vacuum that alternative and sometimes unreliable sources fill, further contributing to the challenges of misinformation and disinformation.

Technology and Deepfakes

Advancements in technology have introduced new challenges to journalistic credibility, particularly with the advent of deepfake technology. Deepfakes, which involve the use of artificial intelligence to manipulate audio and video content, can create convincing but entirely fabricated media. This raises concerns about the authenticity of visual and auditory evidence, challenging journalists to develop new methods for verifying information in an era where seeing is no longer necessarily believing.

Rebuilding Credibility

Rebuilding credibility requires a multifaceted approach that addresses both internal and external factors. Journalistic integrity, fact-checking, and transparency in reporting are essential elements in regaining the public's trust. Media organizations must also be proactive in addressing errors and issuing corrections promptly. Collaborations with fact-checking organizations and adherence to established ethical guidelines can contribute to a more credible and trustworthy journalism landscape.

The Decline of Traditional Media

The decline of traditional media, including newspapers and broadcast television, poses another formidable challenge to the journalism industry. The rise of digital platforms, changes in consumer behavior, and economic pressures have reshaped the media landscape, leading to a reevaluation of the traditional business models that sustained journalism for centuries.

Digital Disruption

The advent of the internet has disrupted the traditional distribution model of news. Online platforms and social media have become primary sources of information for many, challenging the revenue streams that sustained traditional media outlets. The 24-hour news cycle, driven by the immediacy of digital platforms, has also altered the nature of news reporting, emphasizing speed over in-depth analysis.

Economic Challenges

Traditional media outlets face significant economic challenges in the digital era. The decline in print advertising revenue, the shift of classified ads to online platforms, and the competition for digital advertising dollars have strained the financial viability of newspapers. As a result, many traditional newsrooms have faced cutbacks, layoffs, and closures, impacting the depth and quality of journalistic coverage. *Cutbacks, layoffs, and closures* refer to measures taken by organizations to reduce costs, often involving a reduction in expenditures, laying off employees, or closing down certain operations or facilities in response to financial challenges or strategic shifts.

Local News Erosion

The decline of traditional media has particularly affected local journalism. Many local newspapers, once vital sources of community information, have shuttered, leaving news deserts - areas without adequate local news coverage. This erosion of local journalism has profound implications for civic engagement, as communities lose a crucial source of information about local government, schools, and issues directly impacting residents.

Adapting to Change

To address the challenges posed by the decline of traditional media, the industry must embrace digital transformation and explore innovative business models. Subscription-based models, partnerships with digital platforms, and philanthropic support are avenues that media organizations can pursue to ensure sustainability. *Subscription-based models* involve charging users a fee for access to content or services, creating a steady revenue stream and reducing reliance on advertising. *Partnerships with digital platforms* mean collaborating with platforms for content distribution, revenue sharing, or technological support, expanding audience reach and revenue opportunities. *Philanthropic support* entails receiving donations or grants from individuals, foundations, or organizations, providing financial support, especially for public interest journalism or non-profit media outlets.

Additionally, efforts to strengthen local journalism, such as nonprofit news ventures and collaborations between news organizations and community stakeholders, can help fill the gaps left by the decline of traditional outlets.

Conclusion

The challenges facing journalism today - bias, credibility issues, and the decline of traditional media - are interconnected and demand thoughtful, strategic responses from the industry. As journalism navigates this evolving landscape, the commitment to ethical reporting, transparency, and a renewed focus on the public interest will be essential in maintaining the integrity of the profession. By addressing these challenges head-on, journalists can uphold their vital role as the guardians of democracy, providing citizens with the information they need to make informed decisions and actively participate in civic life.

Chapter 7. Ethics in News Gathering
Protecting Sources, Avoiding Conflicts of Interest, and Maintaining Objectivity

Introduction

In the ever-evolving landscape of journalism, the ethical principles that guide news gathering play a crucial role in maintaining the integrity and credibility of the profession. This article delves into the essential aspects of ethics in news gathering, with a focus on protecting sources, avoiding conflicts of interest, and maintaining objectivity. As the fourth estate, journalists bear the responsibility of being the watchdogs of society, and adherence to ethical standards is paramount to fulfilling this role.

Protecting Sources

One of the cornerstones of journalism ethics is the protection of sources. Journalists often rely on confidential informants, whistleblowers, or individuals who fear reprisal for sharing sensitive information. Ensuring the safety and anonymity of these sources is not just an ethical imperative but also a legal requirement in many jurisdictions.

1. Confidentiality and Trust

Journalists must establish a relationship of trust with their sources. This involves assuring sources that their identities will be protected, and information will be handled with the utmost confidentiality. Maintaining this trust is essential for the journalist-source relationship to endure.

2. Legal Protections

In many countries, laws exist to shield journalists from legal actions aimed at forcing them to disclose their sources. Journalists, in turn, must be aware of these legal protections and be prepared to defend their sources if necessary. This legal framework serves as a safeguard, reinforcing the ethical obligation to protect sources.

3. Balancing Transparency

While protecting sources is crucial, journalists must also navigate the delicate balance between confidentiality and transparency. Ethical journalism calls for a careful consideration of when to grant anonymity and when to reveal sources, weighing the public interest against the need to protect individuals who provide valuable information.

Avoiding Conflicts of Interest

Conflicts of interest can compromise the impartiality and credibility of journalistic work. Maintaining objectivity requires journalists to be vigilant in identifying and managing potential conflicts that may arise during the news-gathering process.

1. Financial Conflicts

Financial ties between journalists and the subjects of their reporting can raise questions about objectivity. It is essential for journalists to disclose any financial interests or relationships that could influence their reporting. Transparency in this regard is key to preserving the public's trust.

2. Personal Relationships

Journalists must navigate the potential impact of personal relationships on their reporting. Close ties with individuals or organizations involved in a story may lead to bias, intentional or not. Recognizing and addressing these personal connections is essential to upholding journalistic integrity.

3. Editorial Independence

Media organizations play a pivotal role in fostering ethical journalism by ensuring editorial independence. Journalists should have the freedom to pursue stories without undue influence from advertisers, owners, or external interests. A commitment to editorial independence helps maintain the public's faith in the media's ability to act as an impartial information source.

Maintaining Objectivity

Objectivity is a fundamental tenet of ethical journalism, demanding a commitment to presenting information fairly and without bias. Achieving and maintaining objectivity requires journalists to be aware of their own perspectives, actively seek diverse viewpoints, and present a balanced narrative.

1. Self-awareness

Journalists must recognize and acknowledge their own biases and preconceptions. This self-awareness is the first step toward mitigating the impact of personal perspectives on reporting. Regular self-reflection and openness to criticism contribute to a journalist's ability to remain objective.

2. Diverse Perspectives

To ensure a comprehensive and objective view of a story, journalists should actively seek out diverse perspectives. This includes reaching out to individuals with varying opinions, backgrounds, and experiences related to the subject matter. A commitment to inclusivity enhances the accuracy and fairness of reporting.

3. Fact-checking and Verification

The credibility of news reporting relies on thorough fact-checking and verification. Journalists must strive to present accurate information, verifying facts from multiple sources before publishing. Rushing to report unverified information can undermine trust and compromise the ethical standards of journalism.

Conclusion

In the ever-challenging landscape of journalism, maintaining ethical standards in news gathering is paramount. Protecting sources, avoiding conflicts of interest, and maintaining objectivity are not just ethical guidelines but essential practices that uphold the credibility and trustworthiness of journalism. As the media continues to evolve, journalists must remain steadfast in their commitment to these ethical principles, ensuring that the public can rely on journalism as a cornerstone of an informed and democratic society. The pursuit of truth and the responsibility to the public demand nothing less than the highest ethical standards in news gathering.

Chapter 8. Whistleblower Protection
Balancing Transparency and National Security

Introduction

In the realm of journalism ethics and challenges, the topic of whistleblower protection stands as a critical pillar supporting the delicate balance between transparency and national security. Whistleblowers play a vital role in exposing wrongdoing, corruption, and abuse of power, shedding light on information that the public has a right to know. However, the protection of these individuals often sparks a contentious debate, pitting the principles of openness against the imperatives of safeguarding a nation's security. This article delves into the complex interplay between whistleblower protection, journalistic integrity, and national security, exploring the challenges and ethical considerations inherent in this delicate equilibrium.

The Crucial Role of Whistleblowers

Whistleblowers serve as the conscience of society, bravely stepping forward to disclose information that would otherwise remain hidden. Their revelations have exposed everything from corporate malfeasance to government misconduct, prompting necessary scrutiny and accountability. Journalism, as the fourth estate, relies heavily on these insiders who risk their careers and personal safety to bring crucial information to the public's attention. Their contributions are integral to the functioning of a healthy democracy, fostering transparency, accountability, and public trust.

Legal Protections for Whistleblowers

To encourage and shield whistleblowers, legal frameworks have been established in many countries. These protections vary, but they commonly include provisions safeguarding whistleblowers from retaliation, ensuring anonymity, and providing avenues for reporting misconduct without fear of retribution. In the United States, for instance, the Whistleblower Protection Act shields federal employees from adverse actions in response to their disclosures. These legal safeguards are instrumental in fostering a culture where individuals feel empowered to expose wrongdoing.

Journalistic Responsibility in Reporting Whistleblower Disclosures

Journalists play a crucial role in amplifying whistleblower disclosures, translating complex information for the public and holding those in power accountable. However, the responsibility of journalists extends beyond merely reporting leaked information. Ethical considerations come into play, demanding a careful evaluation of the potential consequences of publishing sensitive details. Striking a balance between serving the public's right to know and avoiding harm is a perpetual challenge for journalists navigating the intricate landscape of whistleblower revelations.

National Security Concerns

The tension between transparency and national security becomes palpable when considering the potential impact of whistleblower disclosures on a country's security apparatus. Classified information, when leaked, can compromise intelligence operations, jeopardize the safety of agents, and undermine ongoing investigations. Governments argue that the need to protect national security justifies restrictions on certain information and the prosecution of those responsible for its unauthorized disclosure. The challenge lies in distinguishing between legitimate concerns for national security and attempts to shield government misconduct from public scrutiny.

The Snowden Dilemma

Edward Snowden's revelations about the extensive surveillance programs operated by the National Security Agency (NSA) in 2013 underscored the complexities of whistleblower protection in the context of national security. While some hailed him as a hero for exposing mass surveillance, others condemned him as a traitor who compromised vital intelligence operations. The Snowden case exemplifies the delicate dance between the public's right to know and the imperative to safeguard national security interests.

Government Response and Prosecution

Governments, faced with the potential fallout from whistleblower disclosures, often respond with legal actions against those responsible. Whistleblowers may find themselves subject to charges under laws pertaining to the unauthorized disclosure of classified information. The legal battles that follow these disclosures raise questions about the extent to which national security concerns can be used to curtail the public's right to information. The prosecution of whistleblowers becomes a battleground where competing interests collide, testing the resilience of legal frameworks designed to protect those who expose wrongdoing.

Journalistic Challenges in Handling Classified Information

Journalists grappling with whistleblower disclosures confront ethical dilemmas concerning the handling of classified information. The duty to inform the public must be weighed against the potential harm that may arise from revealing sensitive details. News organizations often engage in extensive deliberations, consulting with legal experts and government officials, to assess the potential consequences of their reporting. Striking a balance between transparency and national security requires meticulous editorial decision-making, sometimes leading to redactions or delayed publication to mitigate harm.

International Perspectives on Whistleblower Protection

The challenges surrounding whistleblower protection are not confined to a single nation; they resonate globally. Various countries approach this issue with different cultural, legal, and ethical frameworks, adding complexity to the broader discourse on transparency and national security. In some jurisdictions, whistleblowers may face more lenient legal consequences, while in others, the penalties can be severe. Understanding the global landscape of whistleblower protection is essential for fostering an informed discussion on the ethical dimensions of reporting sensitive information.

Technological Advances and Whistleblower Vulnerabilities

As technology evolves, so do the methods used by governments and corporations to protect classified information. Simultaneously, whistleblowers leverage technology to disseminate information anonymously. The digital age has brought about both opportunities and challenges. Secure communication channels allow for the anonymous transmission of information, protecting whistleblowers from immediate detection. However, advancements in surveillance technologies also pose a threat to anonymity, raising concerns about the safety of those who come forward with sensitive information.

Conclusion

Whistleblower protection occupies a central space in the ongoing dialogue about journalism ethics and challenges. It is a realm where the principles of transparency, accountability, and national security intersect, creating a complex landscape for journalists, governments, and the public. As the world grapples with the intricacies of balancing the public's right to know and safeguarding sensitive information, ongoing discussions, legal reforms, and ethical considerations will shape the future of whistleblower protection. The delicate equilibrium between transparency and national security demands a nuanced approach, one that upholds the values of democracy while recognizing the legitimate imperatives of safeguarding a nation's security.

Chapter 9. Investigative Journalism
Uncovering the Truth and Exposing Corruption

Introduction

In the realm of journalism, investigative reporting stands as a beacon of truth-seeking and accountability. It is a form of journalism that goes beyond the surface, delving deep into the core of issues to uncover hidden truths, expose corruption, and hold those in power accountable. In this article, we explore the significance of investigative journalism, its challenges, and its ethical dimensions.

Investigative journalism is the cornerstone of a healthy democracy. It serves as a watchdog, scrutinizing the actions of governments, corporations, and individuals. The primary objective is to unearth information that would otherwise remain concealed, bringing to light stories that have the potential to reshape societies and institutions. Investigative journalists act as the voice of the voiceless, challenging the powerful and ensuring transparency in the public interest.

The Role of Investigative Journalism in Society

1. Shaping Public Discourse

Investigative journalism plays a pivotal role in shaping public discourse. By delving into complex issues and presenting well-researched narratives, investigative reporters inform the public and encourage critical thinking. They bridge the gap between information and understanding, empowering citizens to make informed decisions and participate actively in democratic processes.

2. Exposing Corruption and Wrongdoing

At its core, investigative journalism is about exposing corruption and wrongdoing. Journalists tirelessly follow leads, conduct interviews, and analyze documents to uncover instances of fraud, abuse of power, or unethical behavior. The exposure of such acts not only serves justice but also acts as a deterrent, discouraging future malfeasance.

3. Holding the Powerful Accountable

One of the primary functions of investigative journalism is to hold those in power accountable for their actions. Whether it's government officials, corporate leaders, or influential individuals, investigative reporters act as a check on power, ensuring that no one is above scrutiny. This accountability is essential for a functioning democracy, preventing the abuse of authority and fostering a culture of transparency.

Challenges in Investigative Journalism

1. Threats to Journalists' Safety

Investigative journalism often puts reporters in the line of fire. Those who expose corruption or challenge powerful entities may face threats, harassment, or even physical harm. The danger to journalists underscores the importance of protecting press freedom and ensuring the safety of those who pursue the truth.

2. Resource Constraints

Investigative journalism requires significant resources in terms of time, money, and manpower. Deep dives into complex issues demand thorough research, which may not always align with the fast-paced nature of newsrooms. Many media organizations struggle with resource constraints, making it challenging to invest in in-depth investigations.

3. Legal Challenges

Journalists engaged in investigative work often find themselves entangled in legal battles. Those exposed in investigative reports may resort to legal action to suppress the story or discredit the journalist. Navigating the legal landscape while upholding the right to free speech is a delicate balance that investigative reporters must master.

Ethical Dimensions of Investigative Journalism

1. Truth and Accuracy

The bedrock of ethical journalism lies in the commitment to truth and accuracy. Investigative journalists must verify information rigorously before publication, ensuring that their findings are based on credible sources and thorough research. Misreporting can not only harm individuals but also erode public trust in the media.

2. Balancing Privacy and the Public Interest

While uncovering the truth is essential, investigative journalists must navigate the delicate balance between the public interest and an individual's right to privacy. Careful consideration must be given to the potential harm caused by exposing personal details, especially when the information does not contribute significantly to the public's understanding of an issue.

3. Independence and Avoiding Conflicts of Interest

Maintaining independence is a cornerstone of ethical journalism. Investigative reporters must avoid conflicts of interest that could compromise their objectivity. The pursuit of truth should be free from external influences, ensuring that the public receives unbiased and reliable information.

4. Providing Right of Reply

In the interest of fairness, journalists must provide the subjects of their investigations with the opportunity to respond. Offering a right of reply allows those implicated in a story to present their side of the narrative, contributing to a more comprehensive and balanced account.

Notable Examples of Investigative Journalism

1. Watergate Scandal

The Watergate scandal, uncovered by investigative journalists Bob Woodward and Carl Bernstein, stands as a watershed moment in journalism history. Their relentless pursuit of the truth exposed the Nixon administration's involvement in the break-in at the Democratic National Committee headquarters, leading to President Richard Nixon's resignation.

2. Panama Papers

The Panama Papers, a massive leak of documents revealing offshore financial activities of prominent individuals and entities, exemplifies the global impact of investigative journalism. A collaborative effort by journalists worldwide exposed widespread tax evasion and money laundering, leading to legal and political consequences for those implicated.

3. Spotlight Investigation

The "Spotlight" investigation by The Boston Globe into widespread child abuse within the Catholic Church showcased the power of investigative journalism to bring about social change. The reporters' dedication to uncovering the truth shed light on a deeply entrenched issue, prompting public outcry and institutional reforms.

The Future of Investigative Journalism

In an era of rapid technological advancements and evolving media landscapes, the future of investigative journalism faces both challenges and opportunities. The digital age provides new tools for research and dissemination, but it also introduces issues such as misinformation and the erosion of traditional revenue models for journalism.

1. Harnessing Technology

Investigative journalists can leverage technology for more efficient research and analysis. Data mining, artificial intelligence, and digital forensics offer unprecedented capabilities for uncovering hidden information. However, ethical considerations must guide the use of these technologies to ensure responsible and unbiased reporting.

2. Collaborative Journalism

In an interconnected world, collaborative journalism has become increasingly prevalent in investigative endeavors. Media organizations and journalists from different countries pool resources and expertise to tackle global issues. This collaborative approach enhances the impact of investigative reporting and fosters a shared commitment to truth and accountability.

3. Sustainability Models

As traditional revenue models for journalism face challenges, exploring sustainable funding models becomes crucial for the future of investigative journalism. Subscriptions, memberships, and philanthropic support are avenues that media organizations can explore to ensure the financial viability of in-depth investigative reporting.

Conclusion

Investigative journalism remains a cornerstone of ethical and impactful storytelling. As societies navigate complex challenges and face threats to democratic values, the role of investigative reporters becomes even more critical. The pursuit of truth, the exposure of corruption, and the accountability of the powerful are essential elements that contribute to a robust and thriving democracy. The challenges may be formidable, but the imperative of investigative journalism in upholding the principles of transparency, justice, and accountability is unwavering. As we look to the future, it is the collective responsibility of media organizations, journalists, and society at large to safeguard and champion the practice of investigative journalism for the betterment of our world.

Chapter 10. The Challenges of International Reporting
Safety, Security, and Cultural Differences

Introduction

In an era of global interconnectedness, international reporting plays a crucial role in keeping the world informed about diverse cultures, political landscapes, and social issues. However, journalists face a myriad of challenges when reporting on international events. This article delves into three primary challenges encountered by journalists in the field of international reporting: Safety, Security, and Cultural Differences.

Safety Concerns in International Reporting

International journalists often find themselves operating in environments fraught with danger. Whether covering conflict zones, natural disasters, or political upheavals, safety concerns are ever-present.

1. Conflict Zones and War Reporting

One of the most perilous aspects of international reporting is covering conflicts and wars. Journalists are exposed to the risks of violence, kidnapping, and even death. The blurred lines between combatants and civilians in conflict zones make it difficult for reporters to navigate safely.

Reporters on the ground must constantly assess the risks and benefits of covering a particular story. Balancing the duty to inform the public with the imperative of personal safety is an ongoing challenge, and journalists often grapple with the ethical dilemma of putting themselves at risk for the sake of reporting.

2. Hostile Environments and Political Repression

Beyond traditional conflict zones, journalists also face challenges in politically hostile environments where freedom of the press is restricted. Governments that suppress dissent may target journalists, subjecting them to harassment, intimidation, and imprisonment. The struggle to report objectively while avoiding retribution from oppressive regimes is a delicate balance that international journalists must navigate.

Security Risks in the Digital Age

In addition to physical threats, journalists today face a new set of security risks in the digital realm. As technology advances, the risks associated with cybersecurity, surveillance, and digital harassment have become increasingly prevalent.

1. Cybersecurity Threats

Digital communication tools and online platforms have become integral to the work of international journalists. However, this reliance on technology exposes reporters to the risk of cyber attacks. State-sponsored hacking, surveillance, and data breaches can compromise the safety and confidentiality of journalists and their sources.

Journalists must adopt robust cybersecurity measures, including encrypted communication and secure data storage, to protect sensitive information from falling into the wrong hands. The constant evolution of cyber threats necessitates ongoing vigilance and adaptation on the part of reporters.

2. Digital Harassment and Online Attacks

The rise of social media has given a voice to individuals and groups seeking to silence or discredit journalists. Reporters covering contentious issues may face online harassment, trolling, and even doxing. *Trolling* involves deliberately provoking and upsetting others online, while *doxing* is the malicious act of publicly revealing and disseminating private or personal information about an individual without their consent. The psychological toll of such attacks can be severe, impacting both the mental well-being of journalists and the quality of their reporting.

International journalists must develop strategies to navigate the digital landscape while safeguarding their mental health. News organizations and media outlets must also take steps to support their reporters in the face of online harassment.

Cultural Differences in Reporting

Cultural nuances play a significant role in shaping the way stories are perceived and reported. Journalists working in foreign countries must grapple with language barriers, cultural sensitivities, and the challenge of presenting accurate and unbiased information to a global audience.

1. Language and Communication Challenges

Effective communication is fundamental to journalism, but language barriers can impede the flow of information. Journalists working in foreign countries often rely on translators, which introduces an additional layer of complexity. Misinterpretation or the loss of nuance in translation can lead to inaccuracies in reporting.

Cultural awareness and sensitivity are crucial for international journalists to navigate linguistic challenges. Building relationships with local sources and understanding the cultural context of a story contribute to more accurate and respectful reporting.

2. Navigating Cultural Sensitivities

Cultural differences extend beyond language to encompass a myriad of customs, traditions, and social norms. Journalists must tread carefully to avoid inadvertently offending or misrepresenting the communities they cover. Sensitivity to cultural nuances is essential for building trust with local sources and accurately conveying the complexities of a story.

Ethical Considerations in International Reporting

In the face of safety concerns, security risks, and cultural differences, international journalists must grapple with a range of ethical considerations. Balancing the pursuit of truth with the safety of individuals and the potential impact on vulnerable communities is an ongoing challenge.

1. The Ethical Dilemma of Intervention

Journalists often find themselves in situations where their reporting could potentially influence the course of events, particularly in conflict zones or areas experiencing political turmoil. The ethical dilemma of whether to remain observers or to actively intervene to prevent harm poses a significant challenge for international reporters.

Decisions regarding when and how to intervene require careful consideration of the potential consequences. Journalists must weigh the impact of their actions on the communities they cover and the broader geopolitical landscape.

2. Protecting Sources and Vulnerable Populations

International reporting frequently involves interactions with sources who may be at risk if their identities are revealed. Protecting the confidentiality and safety of sources is a paramount ethical concern. Moreover, journalists must navigate the potential impact of their reporting on vulnerable populations, ensuring that their work does not exacerbate existing tensions or contribute to harm.

Conclusion

The challenges of international reporting encompass a complex interplay of safety, security, and cultural differences. Journalists operating in this dynamic environment must continually adapt to new threats and ethical considerations. As the world becomes increasingly interconnected, the importance of accurate and nuanced international reporting cannot be overstated. News organizations, journalists, and the broader public must work together to address these challenges, fostering a global media landscape that prioritizes truth, safety, and cultural understanding.

Chapter 11. Press Freedom and Censorship
Fighting for the Right to Report

Introduction

In the realm of journalism, the principles of press freedom and censorship represent a delicate balance that often defines the ethical landscape of the profession. The role of journalists as watchdogs of democracy is integral to the functioning of a free society, and yet, this very role is frequently challenged by the specter of censorship. This article delves into the complex interplay between press freedom and censorship, exploring the challenges faced by journalists in upholding their right to report.

The Historical Struggle for Press Freedom

The history of press freedom is replete with instances where journalists have fought against oppressive regimes and authoritarian rulers to ensure the dissemination of information. From the printing press revolution to the modern digital age, the struggle for a free press has been an ongoing battle. The notion that the press serves as the Fourth Estate, holding those in power accountable, has been a driving force behind this historical struggle.

1. The Printing Press Revolution: Birth of Press Freedom

The invention of the printing press in the 15th century marked a turning point in the history of press freedom. With the ability to mass-produce written material, information became more accessible to the public, challenging the hegemony of monarchs and religious authorities. However, even as the press gained prominence, it often faced censorship from ruling powers keen on controlling the narrative.

2. The Enlightenment Era: Ideas, Information, and Press Freedom

The Enlightenment era, spanning the late 17th to 18th centuries, championed reason, science, and individual rights, fostering critical thinking and influencing societal and political changes in Europe. Key ideas included liberty, equality, and the pursuit of knowledge.

The Enlightenment era further fueled the ideals of press freedom. Thinkers like John Milton and John Locke championed the importance of a free press in shaping public opinion and fostering an informed citizenry. These ideas laid the groundwork for the democratic principles that underpin many societies today. Nevertheless, the struggle for press freedom persisted in the face of political and religious censorship.

Press Freedom in the Modern Context

While the battles of the past have significantly shaped the foundations of press freedom, contemporary journalists continue to grapple with challenges that threaten their ability to report without restraint. In the modern context, the struggle for press freedom is often entwined with issues such as political interference, technological advancements, and the evolving nature of information dissemination.

1. Political Interference: A Threat to Press Freedom

In many parts of the world, journalists find themselves in the crosshairs of political interference. Governments, both democratic and authoritarian, may attempt to control the narrative by suppressing unfavorable information or manipulating public discourse. Press freedom becomes a casualty when journalists face threats, harassment, or imprisonment for their reporting.

2. Technological Challenges: Navigating the Digital Landscape

The advent of the internet and digital media has revolutionized the way information is disseminated. While this has opened up new avenues for journalism, it has also presented challenges. Online censorship, restrictions on social media, and the spread of misinformation pose significant hurdles to journalists striving to maintain the integrity of their reporting.

Censorship: Forms and Implications

Censorship takes various forms, each with its own set of implications for press freedom. From overt government control to subtle self-censorship, journalists navigate a complex terrain where the threat to free expression can arise from multiple sources.

1. Government Censorship: The Iron Fist of Authority

In authoritarian regimes, government censorship is a blunt instrument used to stifle dissent and control the narrative. Laws restricting freedom of the press, censorship boards, and punitive measures against journalists are wielded to maintain a tight grip on information. The consequences for journalists can range from job loss to imprisonment, creating an atmosphere of fear that hampers investigative journalism.

2. Self-Censorship: The Subtle Stranglehold

While government censorship is often overt, self-censorship operates more subtly. Journalists, cognizant of potential repercussions, may choose to withhold or alter information to avoid conflict or backlash. This form of censorship can be insidious, as it erodes the foundational principles of journalism from within. The fear of economic consequences or personal safety can lead to a chilling effect, stifling the robust exchange of ideas that a free press requires.

Global Perspectives on Press Freedom

Press freedom is a global concern, and the challenges faced by journalists vary widely across different regions. Examining the state of press freedom in various parts of the world provides valuable insights into the complex web of factors influencing the ability of journalists to report without fear of censorship.

1. Challenges in Authoritarian Regimes: The Struggle for a Voice

In countries with authoritarian regimes, the battle for press freedom is often an uphill struggle. Journalists face censorship, harassment, and imprisonment as they attempt to shine a light on government actions. The international community plays a crucial role in advocating for the rights of journalists in such environments, calling attention to human rights abuses and pressuring oppressive regimes to loosen their grip on information.

2. Press Freedom in Democracies: Balancing Act

Even in democracies, press freedom is not guaranteed. Economic pressures, corporate interests, and political affiliations can influence media organizations, leading to biased reporting or the suppression of certain perspectives. Journalists must navigate a delicate balance, upholding their ethical duty to report truthfully while contending with the commercial and political considerations that often shape media landscapes in democratic societies.

The Role of Technology in Press Freedom

As technology continues to evolve, its impact on press freedom becomes increasingly significant. While the digital age has empowered journalists with new tools for information dissemination, it has also introduced challenges that can be exploited for the suppression of free expression.

1. Internet Censorship: Navigating the Virtual Minefield

Governments, particularly in authoritarian regimes, may employ tactics to censor online content, limiting access to information and stifling dissent. The use of firewalls, content filtering, and targeted cyberattacks on media outlets pose formidable challenges to journalists operating in the digital realm. Efforts to circumvent such censorship often involve technological ingenuity and collaboration with global advocacy groups.

2. Social Media and Disinformation: A Double-Edged Sword

While social media platforms offer a democratized space for information sharing, they also present challenges related to disinformation and manipulation. The spread of false narratives, the rise of echo chambers, and the weaponization of information for political purposes threaten the credibility of journalism. The *weaponization of information* refers to the intentional use of information, often through disinformation or propaganda, to manipulate public opinion, influence political events, or achieve strategic objectives. This tactic exploits media and communication channels to spread misleading or false narratives for political or ideological gain. Journalists must navigate this complex landscape, striving to uphold ethical standards while combating the viral spread of misinformation.

The Ethical Imperative: Navigating Press Freedom Challenges

In the face of mounting challenges, journalists must adhere to ethical principles that underpin their profession. Navigating the delicate balance between press freedom and censorship requires a commitment to truth, integrity, and the public's right to know.

1. Journalistic Integrity: Upholding the Truth

Maintaining journalistic integrity is paramount in the face of external pressures. Journalists must adhere to ethical guidelines, fact-check rigorously, and present information fairly and accurately. The credibility of the press hinges on its commitment to the truth, even when faced with attempts to suppress or distort information.

2. Solidarity and Advocacy: Strengthening the Press Community

In the fight for press freedom, solidarity among journalists and media organizations is crucial. Advocacy groups, both local and international, play a pivotal role in supporting journalists under threat and holding oppressive regimes accountable. Strengthening the global press community creates a united front against censorship, fostering an environment where the free exchange of ideas can thrive.

Conclusion

Press freedom and censorship are intertwined forces that shape the landscape of journalism. The historical struggle for press freedom, the challenges faced by journalists in the modern context, and the ethical imperatives that guide their work underscore the importance of a free press in upholding democratic values. As we navigate an ever-evolving media landscape, the fight for the right to report remains a fundamental battle, one that requires unwavering commitment to the principles that underpin the integrity of journalism. The press, as the guardian of truth, must continue to push against the constraints of censorship, ensuring that the public's right to information prevails in the face of adversity.

Chapter 12. Environmental Journalism
Navigating Ethical Considerations in Reporting on Climate and Sustainability

Introduction

Environmental journalism plays a pivotal role in shaping public opinion and awareness about critical issues surrounding climate change and sustainability. As the world grapples with the consequences of environmental degradation, journalists find themselves at the forefront, tasked with the responsibility of communicating complex scientific information to the public. However, this noble pursuit is not without its challenges, as ethical considerations loom large in the field of environmental journalism. This article explores the ethical dimensions that journalists must navigate when reporting on climate and sustainability, examining issues ranging from bias and sensationalism to the delicate balance between advocacy and objectivity.

The Challenge of Objectivity

One of the fundamental ethical considerations in environmental journalism is the pursuit of objectivity. Journalists are tasked with presenting information fairly and without bias, allowing the audience to form their own opinions. However, in the realm of environmental reporting, achieving true objectivity can be challenging. The urgency and severity of climate change can tempt journalists to adopt a more advocacy-oriented approach. Striking the right balance between informing the public and avoiding undue alarmism or skepticism is a delicate dance that environmental journalists must master.

Sensationalism vs. Accuracy

Environmental issues often involve complex scientific data that can be difficult to convey in a way that engages the public without resorting to sensationalism. While the desire to capture attention is natural, journalists must tread carefully to avoid exaggeration or oversimplification of facts. Sensationalism not only erodes public trust but also undermines the credibility of environmental journalism as a whole. Striving for accuracy and clarity is essential in ensuring that the public is well-informed without succumbing to the pitfalls of sensationalistic reporting.

Balancing Advocacy and Journalism

Advocacy involves actively supporting a cause with a clear agenda, while journalism is the unbiased practice of gathering, verifying, and presenting news and information to the public. The relationship between advocacy and journalism is a contentious one in environmental reporting. While some argue that journalists should remain impartial observers, others believe that the severity of environmental issues requires a more activist stance. Striking the right balance is crucial, as overly biased reporting can alienate audiences, while a lack of advocacy may fail to convey the urgency of the environmental challenges we face. Journalists must navigate this ethical tightrope, weighing the need for objectivity against the responsibility to drive positive change.

Scientific Complexity and Simplification

Climate change and sustainability are inherently complex topics, often involving intricate scientific details. Communicating this complexity to a broad audience requires a delicate touch. Journalists must strike a balance between accuracy and accessibility, avoiding the temptation to oversimplify or omit critical information. Ethical reporting demands a commitment to conveying the nuances of environmental issues, even when faced with the challenge of making complex scientific concepts understandable to a diverse readership.

Addressing Bias in Environmental Reporting

Bias is an ever-present concern in journalism, and environmental reporting is no exception. Journalists must be vigilant in identifying and mitigating their own biases, whether political, economic, or cultural, to ensure fair and balanced reporting. Addressing bias also extends to the selection of sources and experts, as an over-reliance on particular voices can skew the narrative. Ethical environmental journalism demands a commitment to diverse perspectives and a conscious effort to mitigate personal biases.

Corporate Influence and Conflicts of Interest

As environmental issues become increasingly entwined with economic interests, journalists face the challenge of navigating corporate influence and conflicts of interest. Reporters must be transparent about potential conflicts and avoid succumbing to pressure from powerful entities that may seek to shape the narrative in their favor. Maintaining journalistic independence is crucial in ensuring that the public receives accurate and unbiased information, free from undue corporate influence.

Long-Term Impacts and Solutions Journalism

Environmental journalism often focuses on the immediate impacts of climate change, but ethical reporting should also consider the long-term consequences and potential solutions. Striking a balance between highlighting the urgency of the situation and exploring viable pathways to address environmental challenges is essential. Solutions journalism in the environmental context involves not just reporting on problems but also showcasing initiatives and innovations that offer hope and inspire positive action. *Solutions journalism* involves reporting on responses to social problems, focusing on constructive and effective solutions rather than solely highlighting issues, to inspire positive change and inform the public about successful approaches.

Engaging the Public Responsibly

Environmental journalists are not merely conveyors of information; they also play a role in mobilizing public opinion and fostering environmental stewardship. Ethical considerations extend to how journalists engage with their audience, encouraging responsible consumption of information and empowering individuals to make informed decisions. Promoting environmental literacy and encouraging public participation in sustainability initiatives are integral aspects of ethical environmental journalism.

Conclusion

Environmental journalism occupies a unique and vital position in the media landscape, tasked with communicating the urgency of climate change and sustainability to the public. Navigating the ethical considerations inherent in this field requires a delicate balance between objectivity and advocacy, accuracy and accessibility, and short-term impacts and long-term solutions. As environmental challenges continue to shape the world, journalists must uphold the principles of ethical reporting, ensuring that the public is well-informed, engaged, and empowered to contribute to a more sustainable future.

Chapter 13. The Role of Journalism in Democracy
Holding Governments and Institutions Accountable

Introduction

Journalism is often referred to as the fourth estate, playing a crucial role in sustaining and fortifying democratic societies. Its primary function is to serve as a watchdog, holding governments and institutions accountable for their actions. In this article, we will explore the vital role journalism plays in fostering democracy, the ethical challenges it encounters, and the evolving landscape of media in the digital age.

The Foundation of Democracy

1. Informing the Public

At the heart of journalism's role in democracy is the responsibility to provide accurate, unbiased, and timely information to the public. Informed citizens are essential for a functioning democracy, as they can make well-reasoned decisions, participate in civic processes, and hold their leaders accountable.

2. Public Scrutiny and Accountability

Journalism acts as a powerful check on power by scrutinizing the actions of governments and institutions. Through investigative reporting, journalists unearth information that may not be readily available, exposing corruption, malfeasance, and abuse of power. This scrutiny is a fundamental aspect of holding those in authority accountable to the public they serve.

3. Facilitating Public Discourse

In a democratic society, open and robust public discourse is vital. Journalism provides a platform for diverse voices and opinions, fostering discussions on critical issues. This exchange of ideas is crucial for the development of well-rounded public policy and for ensuring that the voices of all citizens are heard.

Challenges in Upholding Democracy

1. Fake News and Misinformation

One of the significant challenges journalism faces today is the proliferation of fake news and misinformation. The digital age has made it easier for false narratives to spread rapidly, undermining the public's trust in the media. Journalists must navigate this landscape carefully, verifying information and upholding the principles of accuracy and truthfulness.

2. Political Pressures

Governments and powerful institutions may exert undue influence on the media, attempting to control the narrative to suit their interests. Journalists often face political pressures, including censorship, intimidation, and legal threats. Balancing the need to report truthfully with the potential consequences of political backlash requires ethical decision-making.

3. Erosion of Trust

The erosion of public trust in journalism poses a significant threat to its role in democracy. Factors such as biased reporting, sensationalism, and perceived conflicts of interest contribute to this decline. Rebuilding trust requires a commitment to transparency, accountability, and adherence to ethical standards.

The Digital Age and Journalism

1. Rise of Citizen Journalism

Citizen journalism refers to the collection, reporting, and dissemination of news and information by individuals who are not professional journalists but contribute to news coverage through digital platforms and social media. The digital age has democratized the dissemination of information, giving rise to citizen journalism. Social media platforms allow individuals to report on events as they unfold, providing alternative perspectives and sometimes breaking news before traditional media outlets. However, this shift also raises questions about the accuracy and reliability of information from non-professional sources.

2. Challenges of Online Platforms

While the internet offers unprecedented opportunities for information sharing, it also poses challenges. The spread of misinformation on online platforms, the echo-chamber effect, and the manipulation of algorithms for political purposes underscore the need for ethical guidelines in digital journalism.

3. Impact of Technology on News Consumption

Changing technology has transformed how audiences consume news. The prevalence of online news sources and the decline of traditional media outlets challenge journalists to adapt their strategies. Ensuring that the public has access to reliable and unbiased information remains a priority amid the evolving media landscape.

Ethical Considerations in Journalism

1. Objectivity and Impartiality

Maintaining objectivity is a cornerstone of journalistic ethics. Journalists strive to present facts without bias, allowing the audience to form their opinions. The challenge lies in navigating personal beliefs and opinions to deliver news that is fair and impartial.

2. Privacy and Sensitivity

Journalists must balance the public's right to know with an individual's right to privacy. Sensitivity in reporting on personal matters, particularly those involving tragedy or trauma, is crucial. Ethical journalism requires a thoughtful approach to minimize harm while fulfilling the public's need for information.

3. Diversity and Inclusivity

Reflecting the diversity of society is an ethical imperative for journalists. Ensuring that different voices are heard, and various perspectives are represented promotes a more inclusive and equitable media landscape. Diversity not only in the newsroom but also in coverage helps build a more comprehensive understanding of complex issues.

Conclusion

The role of journalism in democracy is multifaceted, encompassing the provision of information, the scrutiny of power, and the facilitation of public discourse. However, this role is not without challenges, including the rise of misinformation, political pressures, and the erosion of public trust. In navigating these challenges, journalists must adhere to ethical principles that prioritize accuracy, fairness, and the public interest.

As we continue into the digital age, the landscape of journalism evolves, presenting both opportunities and obstacles. The rise of citizen journalism and the impact of technology on news consumption underscore the need for a commitment to ethical reporting practices. Journalism, as the guardian of democracy, must adapt to the changing times while upholding the values that underpin its essential role in society. Only through a steadfast commitment to truth, accountability, and the public interest can journalism fulfill its duty as a cornerstone of democratic governance.

Chapter 14. Ethics in Opinion Writing
Balancing Freedom of Expression with Responsibility

Introduction

Opinion writing plays a pivotal role in shaping public discourse, offering diverse perspectives, and fostering democratic dialogue. However, with great power comes great responsibility, and this adage holds true in the realm of journalism, where the ethical considerations of expressing opinions are paramount. In this article, we will delve into the intricacies of ethics in opinion writing, exploring the delicate balance between the freedom of expression and the responsibility that accompanies it.

The Essence of Opinion Writing

Opinion writing involves expressing personal viewpoints, analyses, or subjective perspectives on various topics, often found in editorials, columns, or opinion pieces within the media.

Opinion writing is an integral part of journalism, providing a platform for journalists and columnists to express personal viewpoints on various issues. Unlike news reporting, which strives for objectivity, opinion pieces are inherently subjective, reflecting the author's interpretation and analysis. This subjectivity, while allowing for a diversity of voices, also necessitates a heightened awareness of ethical considerations.

Freedom of Expression: A Fundamental Right

Freedom of expression is a cornerstone of democratic societies, enabling individuals to articulate their thoughts and ideas without fear of censorship. In the context of opinion writing, this freedom empowers journalists to express their perspectives openly, contributing to the marketplace of ideas. However, this freedom is not absolute and must be exercised with a keen understanding of its implications on public discourse.

The Power of Influence

Opinion writers wield a significant influence over their readership, shaping public opinion and attitudes. This influence is a double-edged sword, demanding a heightened sense of responsibility from writers. Journalists must be cognizant of the potential impact of their words on the audience and strive to maintain ethical standards in their writing.

Objectivity vs. Subjectivity

While news reporting strives for objectivity, opinion writing embraces subjectivity. Navigating this fine line requires journalists to be transparent about their biases and affiliations. Readers have the right to be informed about the author's perspective, allowing them to critically assess the opinions presented. This transparency fosters trust and enhances the ethical integrity of opinion pieces.

Avoiding Sensationalism

In the pursuit of readership and engagement, some opinion writers may succumb to sensationalism. Sensationalized content, while capturing attention, can undermine the ethical principles of responsible journalism. Opinion writers must resist the temptation to exaggerate or manipulate facts for dramatic effect, prioritizing accuracy and fairness in their narratives.

The Duty of Verification

Opinion writing does not absolve journalists from the duty of verification. Even though opinions are subjective, the underlying facts and information must be accurate. Misrepresentation of facts not only erodes the credibility of the writer but also undermines the trust of the audience. Journalists must diligently fact-check and verify information before presenting their opinions to the public.

Distinguishing Between Fact and Opinion

Readers often rely on journalists to help them distinguish between fact and opinion. Opinion writers should be clear in delineating between the two, avoiding the blurring of lines that could lead to misinformation. Presenting well-reasoned arguments based on factual information enhances the credibility of the opinion piece.

Addressing Controversial Topics

Opinion writing frequently involves addressing controversial and sensitive topics. While writers have the right to express dissenting opinions, they must do so responsibly, avoiding hate speech or the incitement of violence. Ethical journalism promotes a healthy exchange of ideas, fostering understanding rather than fueling animosity.

Engaging in Constructive Criticism

Constructive criticism is a hallmark of responsible opinion writing. Journalists have a duty to criticize policies, actions, and individuals when warranted, but this criticism should be grounded in thoughtful analysis and a commitment to improvement. Personal attacks and unfounded accusations detract from the ethical foundations of journalism.

Balancing Conflicting Ethical Principles

Ethics in opinion writing often involves navigating conflicting principles, such as the tension between freedom of expression and the potential harm caused by inflammatory rhetoric. Striking a balance requires careful consideration of the societal impact of opinions, weighing the benefits of diverse perspectives against the potential harm caused by irresponsible expression.

Accountability and Corrections

When errors in judgment or fact emerge, opinion writers must be accountable for their work. Transparently acknowledging mistakes and promptly issuing corrections upholds the integrity of the journalistic profession. Failure to do so not only damages the reputation of the writer but also erodes the public's trust in journalism as a whole.

Conclusion

In the ever-evolving landscape of journalism, the ethics of opinion writing remain a critical area of concern. Balancing the freedom of expression with the responsibility to the public requires a nuanced understanding of the power and influence wielded by opinion writers. As custodians of the fourth estate, journalists must uphold the highest ethical standards, fostering a robust and informed public discourse that contributes positively to the democratic ideals we hold dear. Through a commitment to transparency, accuracy, and constructive engagement, opinion writers can play a vital role in shaping a society that values both the diversity of voices and the ethical responsibilities inherent in expressing opinions.

Chapter 15. The Ethics of Photojournalism
When Images Can Be More Powerful than Words

Introduction

Photojournalism is a form of journalism that utilizes images, typically photographs, to tell news stories and convey information, capturing and presenting visual narratives of events, issues, and human experiences. In the realm of journalism, the power of storytelling lies not only in words but also in visuals. Photojournalism, a distinct and impactful form of storytelling, often captures the essence of an event or issue in a single frame. However, with this power comes great responsibility. The ethical considerations surrounding photojournalism are complex and multifaceted, requiring a delicate balance between the pursuit of truth and the potential harm that images can inflict. This article delves into the ethical dimensions of photojournalism, exploring the challenges faced by photographers and the impact of their work on society.

The Responsibility of Truth

One of the primary ethical imperatives in journalism, including photojournalism, is the pursuit of truth. Images have the ability to convey a reality that words may fall short of capturing. Photographers, as visual storytellers, carry the responsibility of presenting an accurate and unbiased representation of events. This truth-seeking mission, however, can be complicated by the subjective nature of photography and the potential for manipulation.

The Dangers of Manipulation

Photojournalists walk a fine line between enhancing the visual impact of their work and manipulating reality. The ethics of photo manipulation have been a contentious issue, with concerns about the authenticity of images presented to the public. The use of editing software to alter the content of a photograph raises questions about trustworthiness and journalistic integrity. While some argue that certain enhancements serve to amplify the emotional impact of an image, others contend that any manipulation undermines the fundamental principle of truth-telling in journalism.

Authenticity in the Digital Age

In the age of digital photography and instant sharing on social media, the authenticity of images is more critical than ever. The ease with which photographs can be altered or staged demands heightened vigilance from both photographers and media organizations. Maintaining the trust of the audience requires a commitment to transparency and honesty. Photojournalists must navigate the temptation to enhance or stage images for dramatic effect while upholding the ethical imperative of presenting an unaltered representation of reality.

The Human Cost of Visual Storytelling

While the impact of powerful images is undeniable, the ethical considerations extend beyond the truthfulness of the content. Photojournalists often find themselves in situations where the act of capturing a moment may exacerbate the suffering of those involved. Balancing the duty to inform the public with the potential harm caused by intrusive or exploitative imagery is a constant challenge.

Informed Consent and Dignity

Respecting the dignity and privacy of individuals depicted in photographs is a cornerstone of ethical photojournalism. Obtaining informed consent from subjects, especially in sensitive or distressing situations, is essential. The challenge arises when journalists must weigh the importance of documenting a moment against the potential harm to those involved. Striking a balance between the public's right to know and an individual's right to privacy requires careful consideration and a commitment to minimizing harm.

The Unseen Consequences

The emotional impact of powerful images on both the subjects and the audience is profound. Photojournalists must grapple with the aftermath of their work, acknowledging the potential psychological toll on those who become unwitting symbols of tragedy. The responsibility to minimize harm extends beyond the immediate act of taking a photograph to the long-term consequences for the individuals captured in the frame.

Navigating Cultural Sensitivities

The globalization of media means that powerful images have the potential to reach a global audience. In this interconnected world, photojournalists must be attuned to cultural sensitivities and avoid reinforcing stereotypes or perpetuating bias. The ethical considerations of cultural representation in visual storytelling are integral to fostering understanding and empathy rather than perpetuating harmful narratives.

Avoiding Stereotypes and Bias

The lens through which a photographer sees the world can inadvertently perpetuate stereotypes or bias. Photojournalists must actively strive to represent diverse perspectives and avoid reinforcing preconceived notions. Ethical considerations extend to the selection and framing of images, ensuring that the narrative presented is fair, inclusive, and respectful of the cultural contexts in which events unfold.

The Role of Editors and Media Organizations

Media organizations and editors play a crucial role in upholding ethical standards in photojournalism. Establishing and enforcing guidelines that prioritize accuracy, dignity, and cultural sensitivity is essential. Providing training and support for photographers to navigate ethical challenges ensures that the entire process, from capturing images to their publication, aligns with ethical principles.

Conclusion

In the dynamic landscape of journalism, photojournalism stands as a powerful means of conveying stories that resonate with audiences on a visceral level. The ethical dimensions of this visual storytelling form require a nuanced understanding of the responsibilities inherent in capturing and disseminating images. Balancing the pursuit of truth with the potential for harm, navigating cultural sensitivities, and respecting the dignity of subjects are integral components of ethical photojournalism. As the world continues to evolve, photojournalists and media organizations must remain steadfast in their commitment to ethical practices, recognizing the enduring impact of images in shaping public perception and understanding.

Chapter 16. The Challenges of Diversity in Journalism
Race, Gender, and Identity

Introduction

In the ever-evolving landscape of journalism, the pursuit of diversity remains a critical goal for news organizations worldwide. As societies become more heterogeneous, the need for media outlets to reflect this diversity in their reporting becomes increasingly apparent. This article delves into the multifaceted challenges that journalists face in addressing diversity, focusing on aspects such as race, gender, and identity.

The Imperative of Diversity in Journalism

Diversity is not merely a buzzword; it is an ethical imperative for journalism. A diverse newsroom ensures a broader spectrum of perspectives and stories, fostering a more comprehensive understanding of the world. However, achieving diversity in journalism is easier said than done.

Race in Journalism

Race has been a longstanding issue in journalism, with underrepresentation and misrepresentation persisting in newsrooms. The challenge lies in breaking stereotypes and providing a nuanced portrayal of diverse racial backgrounds. News organizations need to actively recruit journalists from different racial backgrounds to ensure a more accurate and inclusive representation of society.

Gender Disparities

Despite significant strides, gender disparities continue to plague the journalism industry. Breaking the glass ceiling remains a formidable challenge, as women often face barriers in climbing the editorial hierarchy. The industry must address these obstacles and create an inclusive environment where female journalists can thrive and contribute to a more balanced narrative.

Intersectionality

Intersectionality is a concept that recognizes and analyzes the overlapping and interconnected nature of various social categories, such as race, gender, class, and sexuality, and how they intersect to shape individuals' experiences of privilege and oppression.

The concept of intersectionality acknowledges that individuals possess multiple identities that intersect and influence their experiences. In journalism, acknowledging and addressing these complexities is crucial. Journalists must recognize the intersectionality of race, gender, and other aspects of identity to avoid oversimplifying stories and perpetuating stereotypes.

Cultural Sensitivity in Reporting

Cultural sensitivity is an essential aspect of ethical journalism. Journalists must be aware of the cultural nuances surrounding the stories they cover, avoiding the reinforcement of biases and stereotypes. This requires a commitment to education and training within news organizations to ensure reporters are equipped to navigate the complexities of diverse cultural contexts.

Newsroom Culture and Inclusivity

The culture within newsrooms plays a pivotal role in fostering diversity. An inclusive newsroom culture is one that values and celebrates differences, creating an environment where journalists of all backgrounds feel welcome. Achieving this involves addressing systemic biases, implementing inclusive hiring practices, and promoting diversity at all levels of the organization.

Addressing Unconscious Bias

Unconscious bias refers to automatic and unintentional attitudes, stereotypes, or judgments that individuals may hold towards others based on characteristics such as race, gender, age, or other social categories, without conscious awareness.

Unconscious biases can seep into journalistic practices, affecting story selection, framing, and sourcing. Journalists must confront and address these biases to ensure fair and accurate reporting. News organizations can implement training programs and guidelines to help journalists recognize and mitigate unconscious biases in their work.

The Role of Leadership

Leadership within news organizations plays a crucial role in driving diversity initiatives. Leaders must prioritize diversity and inclusion, setting an example for the rest of the newsroom. This involves not only hiring practices but also promoting a culture that values diverse perspectives and voices.

Ethical Considerations in Diverse Storytelling

Ethical considerations become even more paramount when telling stories that involve diversity. Journalists must navigate the fine line between shedding light on underrepresented issues and avoiding exploitation or tokenization. *Tokenization* refers to the risk of treating certain individuals or issues as mere symbols or tokens, rather than addressing their complexity, experiences, or challenges authentically. Journalists must balance the task of bringing attention to underrepresented issues with the responsibility to avoid exploitation or reduction of those issues to symbolic gestures. This requires a commitment to accuracy, sensitivity, and a deep understanding of the communities being covered.

The Impact of Diverse Journalism on Audience Trust

Diverse journalism encompasses the practice of reporting that actively includes and represents a variety of perspectives, voices, and experiences, aiming to reflect the rich diversity of communities and address underrepresented narratives in media coverage. Diverse journalism has a direct impact on audience trust. When news organizations accurately represent the diverse reality of their communities, audiences are more likely to trust the information they provide. This trust is a cornerstone of journalism ethics and underscores the importance of prioritizing diversity in newsrooms.

Conclusion

The challenges of diversity in journalism are complex and multifaceted, requiring a concerted effort from news organizations, journalists, and industry leaders. By addressing issues related to race, gender, and identity, the journalism industry can move towards a more inclusive and representative future. The imperative is not just ethical; it is essential for the industry's credibility and its ability to serve diverse audiences in an ever-changing world.

Chapter 17. Media Literacy Education
Promoting Critical Thinking in News Consumption

Introduction

Media literacy education has become increasingly crucial in the digital age, where information is abundant, and the lines between fact and fiction can blur easily. As technology continues to advance, the need for individuals to develop critical thinking skills in news consumption becomes imperative. This article explores the significance of media literacy education in the context of journalism ethics and challenges, emphasizing its role in fostering critical thinking among consumers of news.

The Evolving Landscape of Journalism

The traditional landscape of journalism has transformed significantly with the advent of the internet and social media. While these technological advancements have democratized information access, they have also given rise to challenges such as misinformation, disinformation, and the rapid spread of fake news. Journalists face the ethical dilemma of navigating through this complex media environment while upholding their commitment to truth and accuracy.

The Rise of Misinformation

One of the primary challenges in contemporary journalism is the proliferation of misinformation. False or misleading information can spread like wildfire, reaching a global audience within minutes. Media literacy education addresses this challenge by empowering individuals to discern between reliable and unreliable sources, identify misinformation tactics, and fact-check information before accepting it as true.

Understanding Media Literacy

Media literacy involves the ability to access, analyze, evaluate, and create media content. In the context of news consumption, media literacy education aims to equip individuals with the skills to critically assess information sources, media messages, and the impact of media on society. By understanding the techniques used in media production and dissemination, individuals can become discerning consumers of news.

Critical Thinking in News Consumption

Media literacy education places a strong emphasis on promoting critical thinking skills, especially concerning news consumption. Critical thinking involves the ability to question, analyze, and evaluate information objectively. In the realm of journalism, critical thinking enables individuals to discern the underlying motives of news stories, identify potential biases, and evaluate the credibility of sources.

Deconstructing News Narratives

One aspect of media literacy education involves teaching individuals to deconstruct news narratives. This includes analyzing the framing of stories, identifying language choices, and recognizing the influence of cultural and social contexts on news reporting. By deconstructing news narratives, consumers can gain a deeper understanding of the perspectives presented and make more informed judgments about the information they encounter.

Spotting Misleading Techniques

Misleading techniques, such as clickbait headlines, sensationalism, and cherry-picking information, are prevalent in today's media landscape. *Cherry-picking information* refers to the selective presentation or extraction of data, evidence, or examples to support a particular viewpoint or argument while ignoring or omitting other relevant information that might provide a more balanced or accurate perspective. Media literacy education empowers individuals to recognize and resist these manipulative tactics. Teaching the audience to be skeptical of sensational headlines and to verify information through multiple sources helps in building a more discerning and informed society.

Fact-Checking Skills

In the era of digital information, fact-checking has become a vital skill for news consumers. Media literacy education teaches individuals how to verify the accuracy of information by cross-referencing multiple sources, consulting fact-checking organizations, and evaluating the reliability of data and statistics. Fact-checking not only promotes accuracy but also acts as a deterrent against the spread of false information.

Ethical Considerations in News Consumption

Media literacy education goes hand in hand with promoting ethical considerations in news consumption. Individuals are encouraged to be aware of their own biases, seek diverse perspectives, and avoid the perpetuation of misinformation.

Understanding the ethical responsibilities of both journalists and consumers contributes to a more responsible and accountable media ecosystem.

The Role of Schools and Educational Institutions

Media literacy education is most effective when integrated into school curricula and educational programs. By introducing media literacy at an early age, students can develop critical thinking skills that will serve them throughout their lives. Educational institutions play a pivotal role in shaping a generation of media-literate individuals who can navigate the complexities of the modern information landscape.

Engaging with News Literacy Programs

Numerous organizations and initiatives focus on promoting media literacy and news literacy. Engaging with these programs provides individuals with the tools and resources needed to enhance their critical thinking skills. Workshops, online courses, and community initiatives contribute to creating an informed and media-literate society.

Addressing Confirmation Bias

Confirmation bias is the tendency to favor, interpret, or remember information in a way that confirms one's preexisting beliefs or values, leading individuals to seek out, recall, or give more weight to information that aligns with their existing views while downplaying or ignoring information that contradicts them.

Media literacy education also addresses the issue of confirmation bias, where individuals tend to seek out information that aligns with their pre-existing beliefs. By promoting awareness of confirmation bias, media literacy initiatives encourage individuals to diversify their sources of information and consider alternative perspectives. This not only fosters open-mindedness but also contributes to a more well-rounded understanding of complex issues.

Media Literacy in the Age of Social Media

The rise of social media has significantly altered the way news is disseminated and consumed. Media literacy education adapts to this changing landscape by emphasizing the unique challenges posed by social media platforms. Individuals are taught to critically evaluate the reliability of information shared on social media, recognize the role of algorithms in shaping content, and understand the potential for the rapid spread of misinformation in online communities.

Conclusion

In the realm of journalism ethics and challenges, media literacy education emerges as a powerful tool in promoting critical thinking skills among news consumers. By equipping individuals with the ability to deconstruct news narratives, spot misleading techniques, and engage in fact-checking, media literacy contributes to a more discerning and informed society. As we navigate the complexities of the digital age, investing in media literacy education becomes essential for fostering a responsible, ethical, and critically engaged citizenry.

Chapter 18. The Business of Journalism
Revenue Models, Advertising, and the Bottom Line

Introduction

In the ever-evolving landscape of journalism, the business aspect plays a pivotal role in shaping the industry's trajectory. As media organizations strive to maintain their independence and uphold journalistic ethics, understanding the intricacies of revenue models, advertising dynamics, and the bottom line becomes imperative. This article explores the symbiotic relationship between journalism and business, shedding light on the challenges and ethical considerations that arise in the pursuit of sustainable financial models.

The Evolving Landscape of Journalism Business

The traditional model of journalism, primarily reliant on print media and subscription fees, has undergone a radical transformation in the digital age. With the advent of online platforms, news organizations have been compelled to adapt to new consumption patterns and emerging technologies. The transition from print to digital has not only changed the way news is disseminated but has also reshaped the revenue models that sustain journalism.

Revenue Models in Journalism

1. Subscription-based Models

Subscription-based models have been a longstanding pillar of revenue for traditional media outlets. Readers pay a fee to access premium content, thereby contributing to the financial health of the organization. However, the challenge lies in convincing an increasingly digital audience to pay for news when free alternatives are readily available.

2. Advertising Revenue

Advertising has historically been a major revenue stream for journalism. Print newspapers and magazines thrived on ad revenues, and the transition to digital platforms brought new opportunities for targeted advertising. However, the rise of ad-blockers and the dominance of tech giants in the online advertising space have posed significant challenges for news organizations.

3. Donations and Philanthropy

As trust in media organizations becomes a critical concern, some outlets have turned to donations and philanthropy as alternative revenue sources. Non-profit models, supported by foundations and individuals who value independent journalism, offer a potential solution to the financial pressures faced by newsrooms.

The Impact of Digital Disruption on Advertising

1. Digital Advertising Dominance

The shift to online platforms has led to a seismic change in advertising practices. Digital advertising, with its targeted and data-driven approach, has become the primary choice for advertisers. Social media platforms and search engines often dominate the digital advertising space, leaving traditional news outlets to grapple with the challenge of attracting a share of the advertising pie.

2. Challenges of Ad-Blockers

The prevalence of ad-blockers poses a direct threat to the advertising revenue model. As users become more averse to intrusive ads, news organizations must strike a delicate balance between generating revenue and maintaining a positive user experience. Ethical considerations arise when publications resort to aggressive advertising tactics to counter the impact of ad-blockers.

Aggressive advertising tactics refers to forceful and potentially intrusive methods employed by publications to counteract the effects of ad-blockers, such as using pop-ups, autoplay videos, or other attention-grabbing techniques. Ethical considerations arise when publications prioritize revenue generation over user experience, potentially compromising user trust and privacy while navigating the challenges posed by ad-blockers.

Native Advertising and Sponsored Content

Native advertising involves seamlessly integrating paid content within a news organization's format, resembling regular news content, while sponsored content is clearly labeled material created or promoted by an advertiser, maintaining transparency about its promotional nature within the news platform.

In the quest for sustainable revenue, many news organizations have embraced native advertising and sponsored content. While these forms of advertising can be lucrative, they also blur the lines between editorial content and advertisements, raising ethical concerns. Maintaining transparency and ensuring that readers can distinguish between news and sponsored material is crucial to upholding journalistic integrity.

Challenges in Balancing Profitability and Ethics

1. Clickbait and Sensationalism

The pursuit of clicks and online engagement can sometimes lead to the creation of sensationalized or misleading content. Clickbait, designed to attract attention and drive traffic, can compromise the credibility of journalism. Striking a balance between capturing audience interest and delivering accurate, unbiased information is a constant challenge in the digital age.

2. Editorial Independence vs. Commercial Interests

The need for financial sustainability often puts editorial independence at risk. Advertisers and sponsors may exert influence on editorial decisions, raising questions about the integrity of journalistic content. Navigating the delicate balance between commercial interests and maintaining journalistic standards requires a vigilant commitment to ethical guidelines.

Innovations in Revenue Models

1. Membership and Loyalty Programs

To foster a sense of community and loyalty among readers, some news organizations have introduced membership and loyalty programs. Loyalty programs involve structured schemes offering incentives or rewards to encourage audience engagement and retention, often through subscriptions, exclusive content access, or personalized benefits based on user loyalty. These initiatives offer exclusive content, perks, and a direct line of communication with the audience, creating a symbiotic relationship that goes beyond traditional reader-publisher dynamics.

2. Microtransactions and Micropayments

News organizations utilize microtransactions, enabling users to make small payments for accessing specific articles or premium features, while micropayments involve minimal monetary transactions for individual pieces of news content, offering alternative revenue models beyond traditional subscriptions.

Micropayments for individual articles or features have gained traction as a potential revenue model. This approach allows readers to pay small amounts for the content they value, providing an alternative to traditional subscription models. However, the challenge lies in convincing users to make these microtransactions consistently.

The Road Ahead: Ethics, Innovation, and Sustainability

As journalism grapples with the dual challenges of financial sustainability and ethical integrity, innovative solutions are crucial. Striking a balance between attracting revenue and maintaining the core principles of journalism requires a multi-faceted approach.

1. Ethical Guidelines and Industry Standards

Adhering to stringent ethical guidelines and industry standards is paramount for journalism's credibility. Establishing and reinforcing codes of conduct that prioritize accuracy, fairness, and transparency can help safeguard the profession against compromising its principles for financial gain.

2. Diversification of Revenue Streams

News organizations must continue to explore diverse revenue streams to reduce dependence on any single model. Combining subscription-based models with advertising, donations, and innovative approaches such as memberships can create a more resilient financial foundation.

3. Embracing Technological Innovation

As technology continues to shape the media landscape, news organizations must embrace innovative solutions. Artificial intelligence, blockchain, and other emerging technologies offer opportunities to streamline operations, personalize content delivery, and explore new revenue avenues.

Conclusion

The business of journalism stands at a crossroads, where the pursuit of financial sustainability intersects with the ethical imperatives of the profession. Navigating this complex terrain requires a commitment to journalistic principles, a willingness to innovate, and a keen awareness of the evolving needs and expectations of the audience. By embracing a diversified approach to revenue, upholding ethical standards, and leveraging technological advancements, journalism can not only weather the challenges of today but also forge a path toward a sustainable and ethical future.

Chapter 19. Collaborative Journalism
Navigating Ethical Considerations in Media Partnerships

Introduction

Collaborative journalism has emerged as a powerful force in the media landscape, breaking down traditional silos and fostering cooperation among news organizations. In an era marked by rapid technological advancements and a shifting media landscape, media partnerships have become essential for tackling complex stories and reaching wider audiences. However, the rise of collaborative journalism brings with it a host of ethical considerations that demand careful navigation. This article explores the ethical dimensions of collaborative journalism, examining key challenges and proposing guidelines to ensure journalistic integrity is upheld in media partnerships.

The Promise of Collaborative Journalism

Collaborative journalism involves cooperative efforts among multiple journalists, news organizations, or communities to collectively gather, analyze, and report on news stories, fostering a shared and diverse approach to information gathering and dissemination.

1. Amplifying Impact Through Partnerships

Collaborative journalism holds the promise of amplifying the impact of news stories. By pooling resources, expertise, and audiences, media organizations can tackle investigations and reporting that would be challenging for individual entities. This collaborative approach allows for a more comprehensive understanding of issues and the potential to drive meaningful change.

2. Diverse Perspectives and Expertise

Media partnerships bring together journalists with diverse backgrounds, perspectives, and areas of expertise. This diversity enriches the storytelling process, offering audiences a more nuanced and comprehensive view of complex issues. Collaborative journalism can break through echo chambers, providing a platform for voices that might otherwise go unheard.

Ethical Considerations in Collaborative Journalism

1. Maintaining Editorial Independence

One of the primary ethical concerns in collaborative journalism is the preservation of editorial independence. Journalistic integrity demands that each participating organization retains control over its editorial decisions. Striking a balance between collaboration and autonomy is crucial to avoid undue influence and ensure that the final product reflects accurate and unbiased reporting.

2. Transparent Communication

Transparency is the bedrock of ethical journalism, and it becomes even more critical in collaborative efforts. Clear communication among partnering organizations and with the audience is essential. Disclosures about the nature of the collaboration, funding sources, and potential conflicts of interest should be made transparently to maintain credibility and trust.

3. Navigating Competitive Dynamics

Collaborations often involve competitors coming together for a common cause. Negotiating competitive dynamics requires careful consideration of how shared information is used and attributed. Journalists must strike a balance between collaboration and healthy competition, avoiding situations where one partner exploits the collaboration for competitive advantage.

4. Informed Consent and Privacy

When working on sensitive stories, obtaining informed consent from individuals involved is crucial. Collaborative projects may involve sharing information across borders, and journalists must be mindful of varying privacy laws. Respecting the rights and privacy of individuals should be a top priority, and obtaining explicit consent for the use of personal information is a non-negotiable ethical requirement.

Guidelines for Ethical Collaborative Journalism

1. Establishing Clear Agreements

Before embarking on a collaborative project, participating organizations should establish clear agreements outlining the scope of collaboration, editorial independence, and guidelines for sharing resources. These agreements should address potential conflicts of interest, funding arrangements, and the division of responsibilities to prevent misunderstandings during the course of the collaboration.

2. Ethics Training for Collaborative Teams

Journalists involved in collaborative projects should undergo ethics training specific to collaborative journalism. This training should emphasize the importance of maintaining editorial independence, transparent communication, and the ethical considerations unique to collaborative endeavors. Building a shared understanding of ethical principles among team members is vital for the success of the collaboration.

3. Audience Engagement and Feedback

In collaborative journalism, the audience becomes an integral part of the process. Soliciting feedback and engaging with the audience throughout the reporting and publication phases can enhance transparency and accountability. It also provides an opportunity to address any concerns or misconceptions, fostering a sense of shared responsibility between journalists and their audience.

4. Regular Ethical Audits

Periodic ethical audits should be conducted throughout the collaborative project to assess adherence to ethical guidelines. This involves reviewing editorial decisions, disclosure practices, and any potential conflicts of interest. Regular audits help identify and address ethical concerns proactively, ensuring that the collaboration maintains the highest standards of journalistic integrity.

Conclusion

Collaborative journalism presents an exciting frontier for media organizations, offering the potential to tackle complex issues with greater depth and impact. However, the ethical considerations involved in such partnerships are paramount. Upholding editorial independence, ensuring transparency, and respecting the rights of individuals are non-negotiable principles that should guide collaborative efforts. By establishing clear agreements, providing ethics training, engaging with the audience, and conducting regular ethical audits, journalists can navigate the complexities of collaborative journalism while upholding the highest standards of integrity. As media partnerships continue to evolve, a steadfast commitment to ethical journalism will be essential in building trust and ensuring the enduring impact of collaborative endeavors.

Chapter 20. Ethics in Data Journalism
Balancing Privacy, Accuracy, and Responsible Interpretation

Introduction

Data journalism has emerged as a powerful tool in the contemporary media landscape, offering journalists new ways to uncover and present stories. Data journalism involves the use of data analysis, visualization, and interpretation techniques to uncover and report on news stories, enabling journalists to explore, explain, and present complex information in a more accessible and compelling manner. However, with the increased reliance on data, ethical considerations become paramount. This article explores the ethical challenges faced by data journalists, focusing on the delicate balance required to uphold privacy, accuracy, and responsible interpretation.

The Rise of Data Journalism

The digital age has ushered in an era where vast amounts of data are generated and made available for analysis. Data journalism harnesses this information to tell compelling stories, providing readers with in-depth insights. The rise of data journalism has been fueled by advancements in technology, data accessibility, and the growing demand for transparency. However, as data becomes central to journalistic practice, ethical concerns have become more pronounced.

Privacy Concerns in Data Journalism

One of the primary ethical considerations in data journalism revolves around privacy. Journalists often delve into personal or sensitive data to uncover hidden stories, but this raises questions about respecting individuals' privacy rights. Striking a balance between the public's right to know and an individual's right to privacy is a delicate task. Journalists must navigate this ethical minefield with care, ensuring that their reporting serves the greater good without unnecessarily infringing on the privacy of individuals.

Case Study: The Cambridge Analytica Scandal

The Cambridge Analytica scandal refers to the controversy surrounding the unauthorized harvesting of personal data from millions of Facebook users by the political consulting firm Cambridge Analytica. The firm used this data to create targeted political advertisements during the 2016 United States presidential election and the Brexit campaign, leading to widespread concerns about privacy breaches, data manipulation, and ethical implications surrounding online user information.

The Cambridge Analytica scandal serves as a cautionary tale for data journalists. The misuse of Facebook data for political profiling and targeting highlighted the potential for ethical breaches in data journalism. This case underscores the importance of obtaining informed consent, being transparent about data usage, and implementing stringent ethical guidelines to protect individuals' privacy.

Accuracy and Data Integrity

Maintaining accuracy is a core tenet of journalism, and data journalists must adhere to this principle while navigating the complexities of data analysis. Inaccurate or misleading data can have far-reaching consequences, shaping public opinion based on flawed information. Journalists must verify data sources, cross-reference information, and employ rigorous fact-checking procedures to ensure the accuracy of their reporting. The ethical responsibility to provide accurate information is heightened in the context of data journalism, where statistical nuances can be easily misunderstood.

The Challenge of Dealing with Big Data

As data journalism often involves handling vast datasets, the concept of big data introduces additional ethical challenges. Journalists must grapple with issues such as data bias, the representativeness of samples, and the potential for misinterpretation. Ethical data journalism requires a nuanced understanding of statistical methodologies, a commitment to transparency about data limitations, and the responsible presentation of findings to avoid reinforcing stereotypes or perpetuating misinformation.

Transparency and Accountability

Transparency is a cornerstone of ethical data journalism. Journalists must be transparent about their data sources, methodologies, and any limitations inherent in their analyses. This transparency fosters accountability, allowing readers to assess the credibility of the reporting and make informed judgments. Journalists should also be prepared to address criticism and engage in a dialogue with the audience, reinforcing the ethical commitment to openness and accountability.

Case Study: The Panama Papers

The Panama Papers is a massive leak of documents from the Panamanian law firm Mossack Fonseca, disclosed in 2016. The leaked documents revealed extensive and often illegal offshore financial activities of individuals and entities worldwide, exposing tax evasion, money laundering, and corruption involving prominent figures, politicians, and celebrities.

The publication of the Panama Papers in 2016 exemplifies how data journalism can uncover widespread corruption and spark global conversations. While the exposure of offshore financial dealings was undoubtedly in the public interest, it also raised questions about the ethical boundaries of data journalism. The responsible handling of sensitive information and collaboration among journalists worldwide showcased the ethical imperative to prioritize public good while minimizing potential harm.

Responsible Interpretation of Data

Interpreting data responsibly is an ethical imperative that extends beyond accurate reporting. Journalists must avoid sensationalism, misleading visualizations, or cherry-picking data to fit a particular narrative. The way data is presented can significantly impact public perception, making it crucial for journalists to prioritize context and nuance. Ethical data journalism involves telling a complete and fair story, acknowledging uncertainties, and steering clear of sensationalist practices that could compromise the integrity of the information presented.

The Role of Editorial Oversight

Ensuring ethical standards in data journalism requires robust editorial oversight. Newsrooms must establish clear guidelines for handling data, provide training for journalists on ethical considerations, and foster a culture that prioritizes integrity. Editorial teams play a pivotal role in reviewing and approving data-driven stories, holding journalists accountable for ethical lapses, and fostering a commitment to the highest standards of journalistic practice.

Conclusion

Data journalism holds tremendous potential for uncovering hidden stories, promoting transparency, and informing the public. However, with this power comes great responsibility. Ethical considerations must be at the forefront of data journalism practices, encompassing privacy protection, accuracy, transparency, and responsible interpretation. As technology continues to evolve, journalists must remain vigilant in upholding ethical standards to ensure that the benefits of data journalism are realized without compromising the principles that underpin the profession. Striking the right balance between the public's right to information and the ethical treatment of individuals' data is an ongoing challenge, but it is one that journalists must meet with unwavering commitment to journalistic integrity and ethical conduct.

Chapter 21. Responsibility in Coverage of Sensitive Topics
Addressing Ethical Challenges in Reporting

Introduction

In the dynamic realm of journalism, the responsibility of reporters transcends the mere act of relaying information. It extends to the ethical considerations that underpin the coverage of sensitive topics. As gatekeepers of information, journalists wield significant influence over public perception, making it imperative for them to navigate the ethical challenges inherent in reporting. This article explores the multifaceted aspects of responsibility in the coverage of sensitive topics, delving into the ethical considerations that journalists must grapple with in their pursuit of truth.

The Power of Media Influence

1. Media's Impact on Public Opinion

The media's role as a shaper of public opinion is unparalleled. Journalists have the power to influence societal perspectives, and this influence is particularly pronounced when dealing with sensitive topics. Whether reporting on social issues, political controversies, or humanitarian crises, journalists play a pivotal role in shaping narratives that can sway public sentiment.

2. Balancing Objectivity and Sensitivity

Striking a balance between objectivity and sensitivity is a perennial challenge in journalism. While objectivity is a cornerstone of journalistic integrity, sensitivity is equally crucial when handling topics that have the potential to cause harm or perpetuate stereotypes. Negotiating this delicate equilibrium requires a nuanced approach that respects the dignity of those affected by the news.

Ethical Considerations in Reporting Sensitive Topics

1. Informed Consent and Privacy

One of the foremost ethical considerations in reporting on sensitive topics is obtaining informed consent and respecting individual privacy. Journalists must navigate the fine line between the public's right to know and an individual's right to privacy. Obtaining consent, especially in cases involving personal tragedies or medical conditions, is essential to uphold journalistic ethics.

2. Avoiding Sensationalism

Sensationalism can be a tempting path for journalists seeking to capture attention in a competitive media landscape. However, the pursuit of sensational headlines at the expense of accuracy and nuance can lead to misinformation and the exploitation of sensitive topics. Responsible reporting demands a commitment to truth and a rejection of sensationalism.

3. Cultural Sensitivity and Representation

Sensitivity to cultural nuances and the representation of diverse perspectives are critical ethical considerations in journalism. Misrepresentation, stereotyping, or cultural insensitivity can perpetuate biases and contribute to the marginalization of certain communities. Journalists must be attuned to these dynamics, ensuring that their reporting reflects the diversity of human experiences with respect and accuracy.

Challenges Faced by Journalists

1. Pressure from Commercial Interests

Journalists often face pressure from commercial interests, including advertisers and media owners, which can compromise the ethical standards of reporting. In the context of sensitive topics, such pressures may lead to sensationalized or biased coverage that prioritizes profit over responsible journalism. Journalists must navigate these challenges while upholding their commitment to truth and public welfare.

2. Social Media and Instant Gratification

The advent of social media has transformed the landscape of journalism, providing new avenues for information dissemination. However, the immediacy of social media can contribute to hasty reporting, misinformation, and the spread of sensitive content without proper verification. Journalists face the challenge of maintaining ethical standards in the face of the demand for instant news.

The Role of Editorial Policies and Training

1. Development of Clear Editorial Policies

Establishing clear editorial policies is instrumental in guiding journalists through the ethical challenges associated with sensitive topics. Media organizations must invest in the development of comprehensive guidelines that prioritize accuracy, sensitivity, and the protection of individuals' rights. These policies should be regularly reviewed and updated to align with evolving ethical standards.

2. Continuous Training and Education

Journalists, as professionals, must undergo continuous training and education to stay abreast of ethical considerations and evolving best practices. Training programs should focus on sensitizing journalists to the impact of their work on individuals and communities, fostering an ethical mindset that permeates their reporting practices.

Conclusion

The responsibility in the coverage of sensitive topics demands a commitment to ethical journalism that goes beyond the mere transmission of information. Journalists must grapple with the power they wield over public opinion and navigate the ethical challenges inherent in reporting on topics that have the potential to shape societal perspectives. Balancing objectivity and sensitivity, obtaining informed consent, and avoiding sensationalism are critical aspects of responsible reporting. Moreover, journalists must confront challenges arising from commercial pressures, the influence of social media, and the need for continuous professional development. By prioritizing ethical considerations, media organizations can contribute to a more informed and compassionate society, where the dissemination of news is not only accurate but also respectful of the individuals and communities it impacts.

Chapter 22. Ethics in Crisis Reporting
Covering Conflict Zones, Disasters, and Trauma

Introduction

In the dynamic field of journalism, ethics play a pivotal role, especially when reporting on crises such as conflict zones, disasters, and trauma. The challenges faced by journalists in these situations are numerous, ranging from personal safety concerns to the responsibility of accurately representing the stories of those affected. This article delves into the ethical considerations that journalists must grapple with in crisis reporting, exploring the delicate balance between providing the public with vital information and respecting the dignity of those living through the crises.

Balancing Accuracy and Sensitivity

One of the primary ethical challenges in crisis reporting is the delicate balance between accuracy and sensitivity. Journalists often find themselves under pressure to deliver breaking news rapidly, but this urgency can compromise the accuracy of the information. In conflict zones, where tensions run high, misinformation can exacerbate the situation. Ethical journalists must prioritize fact-checking and verification processes to ensure that their reporting is both timely and reliable.

Additionally, sensitivity in reporting is crucial, especially when dealing with traumatic events. Journalists must be mindful of the emotional toll their coverage may have on survivors, families, and communities. Striking the right balance between accuracy and sensitivity requires a nuanced approach, emphasizing the importance of responsible storytelling that considers the human impact of the crisis.

Informed Consent and Privacy Concerns

Respecting the privacy and dignity of individuals affected by crises is an essential aspect of ethical journalism. Obtaining informed consent from those featured in stories is a fundamental ethical obligation. In crisis reporting, journalists must navigate the challenging terrain of obtaining consent in situations where people may be distressed, vulnerable, or in shock.

While the public has a right to know about important events, journalists must weigh this against the potential harm caused by intrusive reporting. Balancing the public's right to information with the privacy rights of individuals requires a nuanced understanding of the ethical considerations involved. Journalists should exercise caution when featuring personal stories and avoid exploiting the suffering of individuals for sensationalism.

Safety of Journalists

The safety of journalists is a paramount ethical concern in crisis reporting. Conflict zones and disaster-stricken areas can be inherently dangerous, with risks ranging from physical harm to psychological trauma. Ethical journalism necessitates a commitment to ensuring the safety of reporters, photographers, and support staff involved in covering crises.

Media organizations bear the responsibility of providing adequate training, resources, and support for journalists working in high-risk environments. Additionally, journalists themselves must adhere to ethical guidelines that prioritize their safety and well-being. Balancing the duty to report with the imperative of safeguarding the lives of those documenting crises underscores the complex ethical landscape of crisis journalism.

Cultural Sensitivity and Stereotyping

Crisis reporting often involves covering diverse communities with distinct cultural backgrounds. Journalists must be acutely aware of the cultural nuances at play to avoid perpetuating stereotypes or misrepresenting the context of the crisis. Cultural sensitivity is an ethical imperative that requires reporters to approach their subjects with respect and understanding.

Stereotyping can lead to biased reporting, reinforcing pre-existing prejudices and damaging the reputation of the communities affected. Ethical crisis reporting demands a commitment to portraying a nuanced, accurate representation of diverse cultures and communities, steering clear of sensationalism or perpetuating harmful narratives.

Impact on Vulnerable Populations

Crisis reporting frequently involves covering vulnerable populations, including refugees, internally displaced persons, and marginalized communities. Ethical journalism requires a thoughtful approach to avoid exacerbating the vulnerability of these groups. Reporters must be mindful of the potential impact their coverage may have on the lives of those already facing adversity.

In some cases, media coverage may inadvertently expose vulnerable populations to further harm, whether through revealing their locations or exacerbating existing social tensions. Ethical crisis reporting necessitates a duty of care towards vulnerable populations, considering the potential consequences of media exposure on their safety, well-being, and access to essential resources.

Accountability and Independence

Maintaining journalistic integrity is a cornerstone of ethical crisis reporting. Journalists must remain independent and impartial, free from external pressures that could compromise the accuracy and objectivity of their reporting. Holding those in power accountable for their actions is a vital ethical obligation, even in the midst of crises.

While access to information may be restricted in conflict zones or disaster-stricken areas, journalists must navigate the challenges of reporting with independence and transparency. Ethical crisis reporting requires a commitment to truth-seeking and uncovering the facts, even when faced with censorship, threats, or attempts to manipulate the narrative.

Conclusion

Ethics in crisis reporting is a multifaceted challenge that requires journalists to navigate a complex landscape with compassion, accuracy, and responsibility. Balancing the need for timely and accurate information with the ethical considerations of privacy, cultural sensitivity, and the safety of journalists is a delicate task. As journalism continues to evolve in the face of new challenges, a commitment to ethical principles becomes increasingly crucial to ensure that the public receives reliable information without compromising the dignity and well-being of those living through crises. An exploration of these ethical considerations in crisis reporting serves as a foundation for fostering responsible journalism in an ever-changing media landscape.

Chapter 23. Trauma-Informed Reporting
Understanding the Impact on Journalists and Communities

Introduction

In the realm of journalism, the responsibility of reporting on traumatic events is an integral part of the profession. Whether it be natural disasters, acts of violence, or societal upheavals, journalists play a crucial role in disseminating information to the public. However, the process of reporting on traumatic events is not without its challenges and ethical considerations. Trauma-informed reporting has emerged as a framework that aims to address the impact of reporting on both journalists and the communities they serve. This article explores the concept of trauma-informed reporting, delving into its significance, challenges, and ethical considerations.

Understanding Trauma-Informed Reporting

Trauma-informed reporting involves an approach to journalism that recognizes and considers the potential impact of news coverage on individuals who have experienced trauma. It emphasizes sensitivity, ethical considerations, and responsible storytelling to minimize harm and prioritize the well-being of those affected by traumatic events.

Trauma-informed reporting is a paradigm that recognizes the potential for news coverage to have a lasting impact on the mental and emotional well-being of both journalists and the communities affected by the events being reported. Unlike traditional reporting, which may focus solely on the

125

facts and immediate aftermath of an incident, trauma-informed reporting seeks to consider the broader implications of the storytelling process.

1. The Journalist's Perspective

Emotional toll on journalists: Reporting on traumatic events can take a significant emotional toll on journalists. Witnessing and documenting human suffering, violence, or disaster can lead to vicarious trauma, compassion fatigue, and other mental health challenges. Trauma-informed reporting emphasizes the need for newsrooms to support the emotional well-being of their reporters.

Self-care and resilience: Trauma-informed reporting encourages journalists to prioritize self-care and build resilience. News organizations are urged to provide resources such as counseling services, debriefing sessions, and mental health support to help journalists cope with the emotional challenges of their work.

Balancing objectivity and empathy: Striking a balance between objectivity and empathy is a key challenge for journalists reporting on traumatic events. Trauma-informed reporting acknowledges the importance of compassionate storytelling while maintaining journalistic integrity. This involves considering the potential impact of language, imagery, and tone on both the audience and the individuals involved in the story.

2. The Community Perspective

Re-traumatization: Traditional reporting methods may inadvertently contribute to the re-traumatization of affected communities. Sensationalism, graphic imagery, and a lack of sensitivity can exacerbate the psychological distress of those directly impacted by traumatic events. Trauma-informed reporting seeks to minimize harm and promote responsible storytelling.

Empowering communities: Trauma-informed reporting recognizes the agency of affected communities. It emphasizes the importance of giving voice to those directly impacted by traumatic events and involving them in the storytelling process. This approach empowers communities to share their experiences, fostering a more nuanced and authentic representation of the events.

Challenges in Trauma-Informed Reporting

1. Balancing Timeliness and Sensitivity

The pressure for immediate reporting: In the fast-paced world of journalism, there is often pressure to report quickly on breaking news. This urgency can conflict with the need for sensitivity in trauma-informed reporting. Striking a balance between timeliness and ethical storytelling is a perpetual challenge for journalists.

Ethical dilemmas in decision-making: Journalists may face ethical dilemmas in deciding what information to include in their reports. Trauma-informed reporting requires careful consideration of the potential harm caused by certain details or graphic content. This decision-making process is complex and may involve discussions within newsrooms about the ethical boundaries of reporting.

2. Dealing with Limited Resources

Time and resource constraints: Many newsrooms operate with limited resources, both in terms of time and personnel. Trauma-informed reporting may require additional time for thorough research, fact-checking, and sensitivity training. Journalists and news organizations must find ways to implement trauma-informed practices within the constraints of their resources.

Training and education: Implementing trauma-informed reporting practices necessitates training and education for journalists. This includes providing resources for ongoing professional development to ensure that reporters are equipped with the skills and knowledge needed to navigate the challenges of reporting on traumatic events responsibly.

Ethical Considerations in Trauma-Informed Reporting

1. Informed Consent and Privacy

Obtaining consent: Trauma-informed reporting places a strong emphasis on obtaining informed consent from individuals who may be featured in news stories. This includes respecting the privacy and dignity of those affected by traumatic events and seeking permission before sharing personal details or sensitive information.

Minimizing harm: Ethical reporting involves a commitment to minimizing harm. Trauma-informed reporting requires journalists to weigh the public interest against the potential harm caused by the disclosure of certain information. This includes avoiding the unnecessary publication of graphic images or explicit details that could re-traumatize individuals or communities.

2. Responsible Storytelling

Language and tone: The choice of language and tone in reporting is crucial. Trauma-informed reporting encourages journalists to use language that is respectful, empathetic, and avoids stigmatizing individuals or communities. Sensitivity to cultural nuances and context is paramount in ensuring responsible storytelling.

Avoiding sensationalism: Sensationalism can undermine the ethical principles of trauma-informed reporting. Journalists must resist the temptation to prioritize shock value over responsible storytelling. This involves refraining from exaggeration, dramatization, or sensationalized headlines that may contribute to the re-traumatization of the audience.

Conclusion

Trauma-informed reporting represents a significant shift in the way journalists approach their work, recognizing the potential impact of news coverage on both reporters and the communities they serve. As the journalism landscape evolves, it becomes increasingly crucial for news organizations to integrate trauma-informed practices into their reporting methodologies. By prioritizing the emotional well-being of journalists, empowering affected communities, and navigating the ethical considerations inherent in reporting on traumatic events, the field of journalism can contribute to a more compassionate and responsible discourse. The challenges are real, but the potential benefits for both journalists and the public make trauma-informed reporting a necessary and ethical evolution in the world of journalism.

Chapter 24. Conclusion
The Future of Journalism and Its Role in Society

As we conclude this comprehensive exploration of journalism ethics and challenges, it becomes evident that the landscape of journalism is undergoing significant transformations. The intertwining threads of technology, ethics, and societal shifts are reshaping the very fabric of how we receive and perceive news. This concluding chapter delves into the future of journalism, considering the challenges and ethical considerations that will define the industry in the years to come.

1. Embracing Change: A Digital Horizon

The digital revolution has propelled journalism into a transformative era, marking a significant shift in the way information is produced, disseminated, and consumed. From the days of print newspapers to the instantaneous dissemination of information through social media, journalism has adapted to the changing times. However, this transition has not been without ethical dilemmas. As newsrooms navigate the intricacies of social media, artificial intelligence, and other technological advancements, the challenge lies in maintaining the core values of truth, accuracy, and fairness. Striking a balance between the speed of digital reporting and the ethical imperatives of traditional journalism will be crucial.

2. Nurturing Journalism Ethics: A Foundation for Trust

Ethics remains the bedrock of journalism, providing a compass for reporters and editors alike. As we move forward, nurturing a culture of ethical journalism becomes paramount. The importance of truth and integrity, highlighted in the introductory chapter, will be the guiding principles that safeguard journalism's credibility. Ensuring that journalists adhere to ethical standards in their pursuit of truth is essential for maintaining public trust.

3. The Role of Journalism in Shaping Public Discourse

Journalism is not merely an observer; it is an active participant in shaping public discourse. The industry plays a crucial role in investigating, informing, and educating the public. In the future, this responsibility will extend to addressing emerging issues such as deepfakes, synthetic media, and other challenges that could distort reality.

Synthetic media refers to computer-generated content, often using advanced technologies such as artificial intelligence (AI) and machine learning. This can include generated images, videos, audio, or other media types that mimic or simulate real human-created content. Deep learning algorithms enable the creation of highly realistic synthetic media, raising implications for various applications, including entertainment, virtual reality, and potentially posing challenges related to misinformation or fake content. Ethical journalism will need to navigate these uncharted waters to prevent misinformation and safeguard the public's right to accurate information.

4. Adapting to the Global Landscape: Challenges and Opportunities

The challenges facing journalism are not confined to national borders. International reporting, press freedom, and censorship are pressing issues that demand attention. As journalism transcends geographical boundaries, ethical considerations must adapt to diverse cultural landscapes. Striking a balance between cultural sensitivity and the pursuit of truth will be a continuing challenge, one that necessitates a nuanced understanding of global dynamics.

5. The Evolving Business of Journalism: Navigating the Bottom Line

The financial challenges facing journalism are undeniably significant. The industry's capacity to provide quality journalism is directly influenced by factors such as revenue models, advertising, and overall financial performance. The future demands innovative approaches to funding journalism without compromising its ethical standards. Collaborative journalism and media partnerships can be avenues for sustaining the industry while upholding the principles of truth and independence.

6. Strengthening Media Literacy: A Shield Against Misinformation

As technology advances, media literacy becomes an indispensable tool for the public. Educating individuals to critically evaluate news sources, discern misinformation, and understand journalistic processes is crucial. Media literacy education must become a widespread initiative, empowering citizens to be active participants in the democratic process by making informed decisions based on reliable information.

7. Diversifying Journalism: Reflecting the World We Live In

The challenges of diversity in journalism, highlighted in a previous chapter, persist as a crucial consideration for the industry's future. Embracing diversity in newsrooms not only promotes inclusivity but also enriches the perspectives brought to storytelling. The industry must continue its efforts to dismantle barriers based on race, gender, and identity, ensuring that journalism reflects the diverse tapestry of the societies it serves.

8. Ethical Challenges in Emerging Fields: Data Journalism and Beyond

The rise of data journalism presents both opportunities and ethical challenges. Balancing privacy concerns, ensuring accuracy, and responsibly interpreting data are essential considerations. As data becomes an integral part of journalistic endeavors, the industry must establish ethical frameworks that guide the collection, interpretation, and presentation of data to the public.

9. Responsibly Covering Sensitive Topics: A Moral Imperative

The responsibility of journalists extends to covering sensitive topics with empathy and consideration. Ethical challenges in reporting on topics such as mental health, trauma, and other delicate issues demand a heightened level of awareness. Journalists must navigate these challenges with a commitment to minimizing harm, respecting the dignity of individuals, and prioritizing the public interest.

10. Preparing for Crisis: Ethical Reporting in Conflict Zones and Disasters

As crises unfold, journalists often find themselves on the front lines. Reporting from conflict zones, disaster-stricken areas, and other high-risk environments requires a delicate balance between the duty to inform and the need to protect journalists' safety. Ethical considerations in crisis reporting involve weighing the potential impact of coverage on affected communities and ensuring the well-being of journalists in challenging situations.

11. Trauma-Informed Journalism: Understanding the Impact

The impact of journalism on both journalists and the communities they serve is an area that requires greater attention. Trauma-informed reporting acknowledges the potential emotional toll on journalists covering distressing events. Media organizations must prioritize the mental health and well-being of their staff, providing resources and support to mitigate the long-term effects of trauma exposure.

12. The Collective Responsibility: Journalism in Service of Society

In conclusion, the future of journalism lies in recognizing its collective responsibility to society. The ethical considerations explored throughout this book serve as a roadmap for journalists navigating the evolving landscape. As technology, societal expectations, and global challenges shape the trajectory of journalism, upholding the principles of truth, integrity, and public service will remain the industry's compass.

Journalism is not a static entity; it is a living, breathing force that adapts to the times. The future demands a commitment to ethical journalism that not only withstands the challenges of the digital age but thrives in it. By embracing change, nurturing ethical foundations, and staying true to the core values of journalism, the industry can continue to play a vital role in fostering an informed, engaged, and democratic society.

As we move forward, let this exploration of journalism ethics and challenges serve as a guide for journalists, educators, policymakers, and the public. By understanding the ethical considerations and navigating the challenges, we can collectively shape a future where journalism remains a cornerstone of a free and enlightened society.

"Journalism Ethics and Challenges" provides a comprehensive examination of the dynamic field of journalism ethics, shedding light on the critical elements that contribute to responsible and credible reporting in today's media landscape. Emphasizing the core values of truth and integrity, the book opens with an exploration of the significance of journalistic ethics. It then traverses through the historical evolution of journalism, addressing contemporary challenges such as the impact of technology and the prevalence of misinformation in the digital age.

The book delves into ethical considerations in various aspects of journalism, ranging from news gathering practices to investigative journalism and the complexities of international reporting. Balancing freedom of expression with responsibility, the narrative spans topics like opinion writing, photojournalism ethics, and the importance of diversity in journalism. Concluding with a forward-looking perspective on the future of journalism, the book serves as an indispensable guide for both aspiring journalists and seasoned professionals navigating the ethical complexities of responsible reporting.

ABOUT THE AUTHOR

Mr. C. P. Kumar is a retired Scientist 'G' from National Institute of Hydrology, Roorkee, Uttarakhand, India. He is also a Reiki Healer and Chakra Balancing practitioner (with pendulum dowsing) and offers Emotional Freedom Technique (EFT) to help individuals with emotional issues. Mr. Kumar has authored many books on technical, spiritual, and social topics.

For further details, you may visit his webpage
https://www.angelfire.com/nh/cpkumar/virgo.html

www.ingramcontent.com/pod-product-compliance
Lightning Source LLC
Chambersburg PA
CBHW071047290526
45795CB00004B/1373